Why Me, Why Not!

by

Chris Sharpe

Copyright ©2025 Chris Sharpe

All rights reserved. No part of this publication may be reproduced, distributed, or transmitted in any form or by any means, whether electronic or mechanical, including photocopying, recording, or by any information storage and retrieval system, without prior written permission from the publisher, except for brief quotations used in reviews or articles.

If you have purchased this book without a cover, please be advised that it is considered stolen property. The book was reported as "unsold and destroyed" to the publisher, and neither the author nor the publisher has received compensation for its sale.

Author: Chris Sharpe
Title: Why Me, Why Not?
ISBN for eBook: 978-1-80623-369-4
ISBN for Paperback: 978-1-80623-372-4
ISBN for Hardcover: 978-1-80623-373-1

Table of Contents

About the Author 4

Chapter 1: Why Me, Why Not! 6

Chapter 2: More Than a Job 26

Chapter 3: Life on the Sales Board! 37

Chapter 4: Always Be Marketing 47

Chapter 5: Leadership Without the Title Owning Influence Before Position 58

Chapter 6: The Daily Grind 67

Chapter 7: Keep Moving Forward 76

Chapter 8: The Real Obstacles 84

Chapter 9: Consistency Wins 96

Chapter 10: Final Thoughts: Why Not You? 106

References 112

About the Author

Chris Sharpe is the real-world renaissance man — a corporate strategist, community leader, and soulful storyteller whose life reads like a blueprint for impact, purpose, and personal evolution. Born and raised in the fast-paced, culturally rich landscape of New York City and New Jersey, Chris learned early on the value of grit, adaptability, and vision. These lessons, rooted in urban hustle and maternal strength, became the foundation for his multifaceted journey. Now thriving in sunny Florida, he seamlessly balances a demanding role at Elevance Health with his responsibilities as a forward-thinking Field Service Representative overseeing smart growth and creating sales solutions for his members.

Chris's leadership style is direct, compassionate, and strategic — grounded in authenticity and driven by results. Whether navigating complex corporate landscapes or guiding a Seminar about Medicare Advantage Plans, he leads with clarity and a people-first philosophy. His community work is not a side project — he is part of Phi Beta Sigma Fraternity, Inc. and holds an MBA. Chris believes that true leadership is about elevating others and creating space for diverse voices, especially in areas where equity and inclusion are overdue.

What sets Chris apart is his remarkable ability to integrate every aspect of his life into a cohesive narrative of impact. He's a husband and a proud dog dad who blends his personal and professional worlds with grace. His daily life could include quoting gospel lyrics and practicing Buddhism that shaped his faith, analyzing stock trends that inform his business acumen, or laughing out loud to a comedy podcast — all before sitting down to dinner. And when the day ends, you might catch him unwinding with a movie — preferably a high-energy action flick paired with popcorn, reminding us that even changemakers need to recharge.

Chris doesn't just talk about success; he's documenting the blueprint. His upcoming book, Why Me, Why Not!, is a bold and deeply personal reflection on navigating corporate America as a Black professional. It's more than a memoir — it's a roadmap for those climbing their own ladders with purpose, integrity, and faith. Through storytelling, he explores leadership, resilience, and the internal dialogue that challenges many professionals of color: Am I enough? His answer is powerful and unapologetic — "Why not?"

A lover of all music genres (with XM radio always nearby), a near-vegetarian who still enjoys the occasional steakhouse ribeye, and a curious student of economic theory, Chris lives life full-spectrum. He doesn't believe in choosing one path — he builds bridges between them.

Driven, grounded, and always evolving, Chris Sharpe is proof that it's possible to wear many hats, hold them high, and walk your purpose — all while lifting others as you climb.

Chapter 1: Why Me, Why Not!

Why Me? The Real Lessons I Learned in Sales

This book offers a personal and professional reflection on the lessons learned through years of experience in sales. What a journey. I have sold everything from cell phones to advertising space for the NY Daily News. While I am not a celebrity or top executive, my journey through the challenges, relationships, and realities of the sales world has equipped me with hard-earned knowledge that can benefit others. Grounded in personal insight and supported by proven sales principles, I aim to provide guidance for aspiring and current sales professionals navigating the dynamic and often demanding career path of sales.

I have even worked for companies that no longer exist. MCI WorldCom. What an adventure that was. I remember selling the new pagers to a lot of the music companies in NYC. Man, people really loved the keyboard format. Having it on your hip. Those were the days. Anyway, from building trust to staying resilient, this book distills my key lessons into actionable advice for those who ask themselves the same question I once asked: **"Why me?"**

Why Me? Owning the Sales Journey

That's the first thing that came to mind when I sat down to write this: "Why me?" Why would anyone want to hear what I have to say about being a salesperson? I'm not a New York Times bestselling author. I haven't been on the cover of *Forbes* or delivered a TED Talk. But I have sat in the parking lots prepping for cold calls. I've smiled through nos, fought through quotas, celebrated quiet wins, and stressed about being let go. I've been on teams that were undervalued, and I've also been part of groups that helped turn things around.

The truth is that my story is one many can relate to—because success in sales doesn't come with titles or luck. It comes with grit, resilience, and heart. And that's the first piece of advice I would give to any new salesperson: own your journey, no matter where you are on it.

Sales isn't about perfection; it's about consistency. One of the biggest myths people have about selling is that it's all charisma and charm. But research shows emotional intelligence, not just personality, is what separates great salespeople from average ones (Goleman, 2006). Understanding how to connect with people—how to listen, respond, and build rapport—goes much further than flashy pitches.

1. Build Relationships, Not Transactions

Early in my career, I thought sales was about numbers. More calls, more leads, more closes. But the longer I stayed in the game, the more I realized it's about people. Me being one of the people. I realized that I should make sure I'm okay first. What do I mean by that? Basically, make sure I get the rest that I need to win for the next day.

If your only focus is hitting a quota, you'll miss the human side of selling—which ironically, is what leads to long-term success. I've had clients who didn't buy from me on the first try, but months or even years later came back because they remembered how I treated them. Don't get pissed off, what God has for you is yours!

Research supports this idea. According to Rackham (1988), successful sales professionals ask more open-ended questions, focus on customer needs, and take a consultative approach. This builds trust and positions you as a partner, not just a vendor.

For me, this meant slowing down and getting to know my clients' goals, pain points, and even their personalities. When you're honest and helpful, people will call you when they're ready—and they'll refer you to others. The trick is not to get lost in the sauce. Don't stay talking about everything and forget that you have other clients and prospects to see.

So my advice? **Be a resource, not a robot.** Follow up without being pushy. Send articles or insights that add value. Show you care beyond the contract. People may forget what you said, but they'll never forget how you made them feel (Maya Angelou's quote still rings true in sales).

2. Master the Follow-Up

If there's one habit that changed my career, it's this: I learned how to follow up. Not just once. Not just after a demo. But systematically, thoughtfully, and consistently.

Most sales are made between the 5th and 12th contact, yet 44% of salespeople give up after just one follow-up (Brevet Group, 2023). That means a majority of people are quitting right before the deal is ready to happen.

The key here isn't being annoying—it's being professional. I created systems to remind me when to check in, what I last said, and what the client cared about. I personalized every message and looked for opportunities to serve, not sell.

Whether it was sending a new solution that fit their updated budget or simply saying "thinking of you" during a holiday, those touchpoints made a difference. I have my members always asking me to send them their yearly calendar if they don't already have it. Every year, I send a little calendar with my card, and folks—let me tell you—it generates referrals!

A strong follow-up process demonstrates reliability, and that's gold in sales. In a world full of broken promises, the rep who shows up consistently becomes the one the buyer trusts. If you're new in sales, don't just make calls—make commitments. And then follow through.

3. Learn the Product, But Speak the Customer's Language

One of the traps many salespeople fall into—me included—is becoming so obsessed with the product that they forget the customer. I used to rattle off every feature, benefit, and bullet point like I was reading a script. But then I realized: **no one buys a drill because they want a drill. They buy a drill because they want a hole in the wall.**

Listen, I have made this mistake a few times and wondered why I didn't get the sale. You've got to find out the potential member's story.

Customers don't care how smart you are; they care if you understand them. Learning how to translate features into benefits that matter to the buyer was a game-changer. I started asking better questions. I studied my industry and learned what metrics mattered to decision-makers. I tailored my language to their level—whether I was speaking to a front-line user or a C-suite executive.

As Cespedes (2014) notes, salespeople must align their message with customer needs and business value. This means avoiding jargon, telling stories, and showing real outcomes.

My advice? Know your stuff—but don't lead with it. Lead with curiosity and then connect the dots to your client.

4. Rejection Is Part of the Process—Not a Reflection of You

If you're going to survive in sales, you need to make peace with rejection. Not easy, Period. There's no shortcut around it. I've been told "no" more times than I can count. I've been ghosted, ignored, and even insulted. But the biggest breakthrough came when I stopped taking it personally. I drove up to a potential member's house on Halloween, and I saw a Black Skeleton hanging from a noose as I pulled into the driveway. I still had to keep it moving,

Every no brings you closer to a yes—if you learn from it. Sometimes it's timing. Sometimes it's the budget. And sometimes, yes, it's your approach. But that doesn't mean *you* are a failure. It means the opportunity wasn't right.

I started treating rejection as feedback. I'd review calls, ask mentors for input, and refine my technique. Over time, I built resilience. Psychologists call this a "growth mindset"—believing that skills can be developed through effort and learning (Dweck, 2006). That mindset helped me push through slow months and hit my stride. Slow times are the weirdest because you're not sure what is happening. Last week I was humming and zipping along, singing a song, and making my sales. What is going on!

To anyone struggling in sales, I say this: rejection doesn't define you. How you respond does. Keep showing up. Keep learning. Keep growing.

Purpose Over Perfection

So, why me? Because I've walked the walk. I've succeeded, stumbled, doubted, and pushed forward. I'm still learning. But I know this much—sales is not just a job, it's a craft. And like any craft, it rewards those who care, practice, and stay the course.

If you're entering the field or thinking of giving up, remember you don't have to be perfect to be powerful. You don't need to have the loudest voice in the room. You just need to be someone people trust, respect, and remember. Show up with heart. Work with integrity. And don't let fear stop you from reaching your potential.

Why me? Because someone like you might be asking the same question—and I've got your back.

Sales Success Without the Spotlight: The Power of Perspective in the Field

Why Me? Why Not?

That's what I bring to the table. A grounded, honest look into the art and reality of sales. I've lived the late nights, the "no"s, the dry spells, and the comebacks. I've been on teams, led initiatives, and figured out how to keep going when motivation fades. And if you're new to sales or wondering if you belong, I want to tell you: **you do**.

Let me help you understand why and how to make your mark without needing to be in the spotlight.

The Importance of Showing Up Consistently

One of the biggest misconceptions about sales is that it's about charisma or being slick with words. **NO!** While those traits might help open a door, they won't keep it open.

What really matters is consistency. I've learned over time that the best salespeople aren't always the flashiest—they're the ones who show up every day, do the work, and stay engaged even when they don't feel like it. **Do the paperwork!** Everybody must do the things they don't like to do!

Sales is a long game. According to Gitomer (2018), "People don't like to be sold, but they love to buy." That means building trust takes time. It's not about pushing a product. It's about being present, following up, remembering the client's birthday, and making sure the order went through correctly.

That attention to detail, day in and day out, builds a reputation you can't buy or fake. The truth is, I've been overlooked plenty of times. But I've also outlasted others simply by being the one who didn't quit.

Consistency builds credibility—and credibility is everything in this business. The worst is when you sign up a new member, then they call you five minutes later telling you to cancel the order.

Listening: The Underrated Sales Skill

If I could teach a new salesperson one thing, it would be this: **listen more than you speak**. If I had listened better, I may have gotten the sale.

It sounds simple, but it's not easy—especially in an industry where we're often trained to pitch. Bite your tongue, rub your face with your hand, put your hand over your mouth—but **don't talk when they are talking!!!**

I've learned that my best conversations come when I'm not talking about what I have to offer, but when I'm genuinely curious about what the other person needs.

A study by Sales Insights Lab (2021) found that top-performing salespeople talk only 43% of the time in sales calls. That means they're listening 57% of the time. Why? Because clients will tell you what they value—if you give them space to speak.

In my own career, I've had meetings where I barely said a word, and yet I walked away with a sale. Not because I dazzled them, but because I made them feel heard. That's the heart of sales—**solving problems, not pushing products.**

When you stop trying to impress and start trying to understand, the whole game changes.

Resilience and Rejection

Here's the part no one tells you about sales: rejection isn't personal, but it will feel personal.

Early in my career, I took every "no" as a failure. I would question my skills, my voice, even my appearance. I didn't understand that rejection is not only normal, it's essential.

I've learned that rejection refines your approach. It teaches you what doesn't work, but it also toughens you up. According to Blount (2017), the ability to handle rejection is one of the core traits of high-performing salespeople.

Every "no" gets you closer to the "yes"—but only if you keep going.

There were weeks when nothing went right. I lost deals. Clients ghosted me. Budgets got cut. But I kept showing up. I kept dialing. I kept learning. That's where character is built—not during the wins, but during the dry spells.

Relationships Over Revenue

Another hard truth: if your only goal in sales is hitting a number, you'll burn out or burn bridges—or both.

The best outcomes I've had came from prioritizing **relationships over revenue**. That doesn't mean you don't want to close the deal. But it does mean you should play a long game.

There's a quote I've always loved: **"People buy from people they trust."** Trust is built over time through authenticity, honesty, and service. I once worked with a client who didn't buy from me until our **fifth** meeting. Five! But when they did, they bought big—and they stayed loyal.

I've sent handwritten thank-you notes. I've made hospital visits. I've called clients just to check on their kids or offer encouragement. Those moments don't show up on a spreadsheet—but they do show up when it matters. Sales is about connection. And when you lead with heart, the revenue follows. Have some skin in the game, spend your own money, and do nice things,

Helping Others Succeed

If someone asked me today, "How can I be good at sales?" I'd say this: Be curious. Be patient. Be relentless. And above all, be yourself. You don't need to copy someone else's style or inflate your personality. You just need to care—really care—about helping people. I remember hearing this from my Director at Sprint back in the day, before they became T-Mobile. "I help people get what they want!"

Sales isn't about convincing someone to do something they don't want to do. It's about aligning the right solution to the right problem. That takes time, intention, and follow-through.

I may not have trophies or titles, but I've mentored teammates, trained new hires, and seen people grow just by applying the same values I live by: show up, listen, serve, and learn. That's my legacy—and it's one anyone can build, with or without a podium.

So, why me? Why not someone more successful or more visible? Because this isn't about being the best on paper, it's about being real, being reliable, and being someone others trust. My story may not be flashy, but it's authentic. And I believe there are more people out there who need to hear this version of success—the one that says you don't have to be a star to shine in sales. I have had so much jealousy and arrows of envy thrown at me that I used it as medicine.

If you're willing to do the work, embrace the process, and focus on people over products, you'll go far. And I'm proof that you don't need to be the number one salesperson in the company to make a difference. You just need to be the one who shows up—with heart, with hustle, and with purpose.

Becoming a successful salesperson isn't just about hitting quotas or landing big deals—it's about resilience, listening, consistency, and relationships.

More Than Just Numbers

Sales are often glorified by images of elite performers, towering leaderboards, and high-stakes deals. But the real story is lived in the trenches—where people like me show up every day to do the work. I'm not a CEO or the top seller on my team. I haven't been featured in sales magazines or stood on podiums. Well, I may have been chosen by one or two of the companies I worked for to be in some of their TV, commercials, and print advertisements. Now that was a two-edged sword. Yes, I got a few more calls, but I also landed more envy and jealousy, too.

The truth is, being a great salesperson is less about status and more about substance. My story matters because it speaks to the 99% of professionals who may never receive awards but consistently create value. I've learned that with the right mindset, tools, and guidance, anyone can grow in this field—and I'm passionate about helping others get there.

Listening First: The Foundation of Sales

One of the most overlooked skills in sales is active listening. New salespeople often think their job is to pitch—when in reality, it's to understand. I help others become better salespeople by teaching them to listen with intention, not just respond with answers. When you truly listen, you hear what the customer values, what they fear, and what problem they're trying to solve.

According to Sales Insights Lab (2021), top-performing salespeople spend 57% of the conversation listening. That data confirms what I've witnessed firsthand: the more I focused on understanding the client, the better the outcome. New salespeople often fall into the trap of over-talking, trying to sound impressive. My guidance helps them slow down and trust the process.

In mentoring others, I encourage questions like "What's important to you about this?" or "What would success look like for your business?" These kinds of questions invite dialogue, and I teach my mentees that curiosity—not charisma—is what drives lasting relationships.

Building Confidence Through Repetition and Consistency

Sales success doesn't happen overnight. Many new reps struggle with self-doubt or fear of rejection. I've been there. But I've also learned that confidence is built by doing the work consistently—not by landing one big sale. I help others understand that showing up daily, refining your process, and learning from mistakes are what lay the groundwork for growth.

According to Gitomer (2018), "Consistency creates credibility." This has been a core lesson I emphasize when working with new salespeople. You don't need to be the loudest voice in the room—you just need to be the most reliable. I teach others how to create habits: setting time blocks for prospecting, tracking follow-ups, and staying organized with customer relationship management (CRM) tools.

I've also helped others reframe rejection—not as failure, but as feedback. Each "no" is an opportunity to adjust the approach. I walk through real examples with mentees, showing how I navigated similar challenges. Through repetition and consistency, we develop routines that make success predictable, not accidental.

Authenticity and Trust Over Transactions

I've learned over the years that customers don't just want solutions—they want sincerity. Helping someone become a better salesperson means teaching them to be real. You can't fake trust. You earn it through honesty, transparency, and follow-through.

Research by Harvard Business Review found that 81% of customers trust companies more when they are transparent (Edelman, 2019). In practice, this means owning mistakes, admitting when you don't know something, and always following up. I teach mentees that while a sale may earn commission, trust earns loyalty—and loyalty leads to long-term success.

In my own career, I've built partnerships that lasted years, not because I was the cheapest option, but because I was consistent, honest, and dependable. I show others how to shift the focus from closing deals to opening relationships. That perspective changes everything. You're no longer trying to sell—you're trying to serve. And that shift is where real sales power lies.

Coaching with Empathy and Accountability

Empathy builds trust, but accountability drives action. When mentoring others, I help them set goals they can measure—number of outreach attempts, conversion rates, or client meetings per week. Then we review their progress together. By combining human connection with data-driven performance, I help others grow with clarity and confidence. I love it when a new salesperson goes out with me to see how I handle a sales call.

I've seen how much people appreciate this balance of empathy and determination to close a sale. They don't need someone to be perfect—they need someone who's been there. I help others become better by being vulnerable myself and showing them what's possible when you combine humility with hustle.

The Power of Perspective

In a profession often dominated by flashy success stories, I offer something different: grounded, steady guidance rooted in experience. My journey isn't about being #1—it's about being there. Being present, prepared, and persistent. That's what I bring when I help others become better salespeople.

If I can pass along one truth, it's this: you don't have to be the loudest, the boldest, or the most decorated to make an impact. You just have to care. You have to listen, learn, and lead with integrity. That's what turns average salespeople into exceptional ones—and that's the kind of growth I'm committed to helping others achieve. Because sometimes, the best teachers are the ones still walking the path themselves.

Helping People Be Better at Sales: A Real Perspective from Corporate America

Sales is one of the most vital roles in any organization. At its core, sales is about connection—understanding the customer, building trust, and delivering value. But for many professionals, particularly those navigating corporate America as minorities, the path to success is rarely linear. As a Black man in corporate America, I've often faced moments when my presence was questioned or underestimated before I even said a word. I don't bring this up to garner sympathy—I bring it up because it's real, and it affects performance, confidence, and opportunity. Why do you think I have a white male on the cover.

Some may say, "Don't play the race card." But the truth is, corporate America has always dealt its own cards. I'm simply acknowledging the hand I've been given. Still, within that reality lies power: the power to perform, to influence, and to help others rise. In this book, I'll share strategies, experiences, and advice that can help sales professionals—especially those who may feel overlooked—become more effective, confident, and impactful in their roles.

The Power of Authenticity

One of the first and most important lessons I learned in sales is that authenticity is a superpower. Sales is not about being the loudest voice in the room or mimicking someone else's pitch—it's about showing up as your full self.

For Black professionals, this can feel complicated. The corporate environment often rewards sameness and conformity. Studies have shown that minorities frequently engage in "code-switching" to fit in with majority norms, which can increase stress and reduce authenticity (McCluney et al., 2019). But I've learned that customers and clients respond best when they sense that you are genuine. That means embracing your story, your voice, and your style.

When I stopped trying to "sound corporate" and started speaking with honesty and clarity, I built stronger relationships and closed more deals.

Authenticity is also about values. If you're selling something you don't believe in, customers can tell. I've always been selective about what I represent because I know my integrity is part of my brand. What is frustrating sometimes is when the product you represent doesn't work the way it was represented. Then, as a salesperson, you must fight for your customer. Call up the various departments to see if you can resolve the issue.

That's a lesson I pass on to every salesperson: never sell your soul to make a sale. Know your worth, know your product, and let that passion speak through your pitch.

Building Confidence in the Face of Bias

Let's talk about the elephant in the boardroom—bias. Whether implicit or explicit, racial bias exists in corporate settings. Black professionals are more likely to report feeling scrutinized or doubted, especially in high-stakes roles like sales, where trust and likeability can determine outcomes (Livingston, 2021).

I've had clients look at my white colleagues first, assuming they were in charge. I've been spoken over in meetings or given the "you're so articulate" line, which, while often meant as a compliment, reveals an underlying surprise at my professionalism. In many Seminars, a lot of the prospects have always said that I look like Denzel Washington. I guess that is good, but I would still like to collect his paychecks. Seriously, being a human isn't easy, and being black makes you jump a few more hurdles.

How do you succeed in this environment? You build confidence like muscle—through repetition, discipline, and self-awareness. Confidence doesn't mean you won't feel nervous. It means you've prepared so thoroughly that even your worst day still meets the standard.

I encourage every salesperson to study their industry, know their clients, and rehearse their messaging until it becomes second nature. Preparation silences doubt—yours and theirs.

Confidence also means learning to advocate for yourself. Don't wait for someone to give you the floor—take it. If your voice isn't heard, raise it. If credit is being misassigned, reclaim it. These are not acts of arrogance; they are acts of survival and strategy in a system that often defaults to excluding you.

Mastering Relationship Building

Sales is not transactional; it's relational. The best salespeople understand that their job is to listen more than they speak. They ask the right questions, they follow up with care, and they become trusted advisors rather than pushy vendors. This is where emotional intelligence becomes your greatest asset.

Being a Black man in America has given me a unique perspective on people. I've learned how to read the room, understand non-verbal cues, and navigate complex dynamics. That awareness translates directly into relationship-building. When you show customers that you see them—not just as potential revenue but as humans with problems you can help solve—you win loyalty.

Empathy is key. So is consistency. I always follow through on my promises. I don't just close deals—I maintain them. Repeat business is the lifeblood of success, and it only comes when people feel seen, heard, and valued.

Mentorship and Giving Back

One of the greatest joys of my career has been mentoring others. I didn't have many people who looked like me in leadership roles when I was coming up. So, I became the person I needed. I take pride in sharing what I've learned—not because I've "made it," but because I've made progress.

Mentorship is especially critical in sales, where burnout and rejection can erode motivation. Research shows that sales professionals who receive regular coaching outperform those who don't by more than 17% (CSO Insights, 2018). I teach new reps to control what they can—effort, attitude, preparation—and to not take rejection personally. Sales is a numbers game, but it's also a human one.

I also encourage minority professionals to build community. Find your allies. Join ERGs (Employee Resource Groups), join a Chamber, or just join a group you like. You never know where your next sale or lead is coming from. Attend networking events and stay connected to people who understand your journey. Representation matters—not just for visibility, but for sustainability. Knowing you're not alone in the struggle makes the wins even sweeter.

Success Redefined

In sales, people often define success by numbers—how much revenue you generate, how many deals you close. But I believe true success is broader. It's about impact. It's about how many people you help, how many bridges you build, and how many doors you open for others.

I've won awards and earned incentives, but my proudest moments are when someone tells me, "You helped me believe I could do this." Or "Because of your advice, I landed the job." Sales is not just a job; it's a platform. Use it to uplift others. Use it to challenge stereotypes. Use it to build a legacy that extends beyond the office walls.

Being a Black man in corporate America comes with challenges that are often invisible to those who haven't lived them. But within those challenges lie lessons that make us better—more resilient, more empathetic, more strategic. Sales is a profession that rewards those who persist, who adapt, and who show up consistently with purpose. My goal is not just to be successful, but to help others—especially those who feel unseen—find their own success. If I can do it, so can you. And if I can help you along the way, then every moment of struggle will have been worth it.

Applying My Sales Experience to Help Others Succeed

A Calling from Childhood

Since I was a kid, I knew I wanted to be in sales. The moment it clicked is still vivid. After school, I would visit my mother, Elaine Daly, at her office at *The New York Times*, where she worked as a marketing manager. She was a single Black mother raising me with strength, grace, and grit. While waiting for her to finish work, I sat quietly, watching people come and go, especially the advertising sales representatives. They wore suits with purpose, walked with confidence, and returned each evening with stories of deals, clients, and wins.

There was something electric about their energy. No one hovered over them, no one micromanaged their every move. I didn't have the vocabulary at the time, but what I saw was freedom. And when someone told me they were paid well, I was sold—freedom and good money. That was the dream.

That early exposure to sales planted a seed that has grown into a career shaped by hustle, resilience, and a desire to help others succeed.

Now, with years of sales experience across industries, territories, and teams, I've come to believe that great salespeople aren't born—they're developed. In this book, I'll share how my journey can help others thrive in sales by focusing on self-awareness, relationship-building, authenticity, and a mindset of continuous growth.

Sales Begins with Purpose and Self-Awareness

Many people fall into sales. I chose it. That distinction matters because people who identify their "why" early in their careers tend to stay motivated through adversity (Sinek, 2009). My "why" was rooted in a childhood vision of independence and value. But as I matured, that purpose evolved: I now see sales as a platform to connect, empower, and drive solutions—not just transactions.

Helping others begin their sales journey starts with a deep sense of self-awareness. Sales professionals who understand their motivations, strengths, and blind spots are more likely to build trust with clients and peers. I encourage new salespeople to reflect honestly on questions like: *Why do I want to sell? What motivates me when times are tough? What value do I offer beyond the product or service?* According to Gardner et al. (2011), authenticity and self-awareness are foundational components of effective leadership, and sales is, fundamentally, a leadership role in motion. You're leading conversations, influencing decisions, and representing your brand.

As a salesperson, coach, and mentor, I often ask sales professionals to think about a personal mission statement. It anchors them, helps them navigate rejection, and brings clarity during tough quarters. Sales is as much about internal resilience as it is about external performance.

The Art and Science of Relationship-Building

No matter whether the product or vertical, sales is built on relationships. Early in my career, I thought being a top closer meant being slick and persuasive. But real success came when I focused more on listening than pitching. Relationships aren't just a means to an end—they're the engine of repeat business, referrals, and long-term impact.

One lesson I always pass on: rapport before revenue. Clients need to feel understood before they trust your solution. That trust isn't built in a single call or flashy demo—it comes from consistency, empathy, and value. Research shows that top-performing salespeople spend more time understanding a client's unique challenges than they do on product descriptions (Dixon & Adamson, 2011).

My experience as a Black man in corporate America has made me particularly sensitive to being misunderstood or underestimated. That's why I emphasize emotional intelligence—being able to read the room, adjust your tone, and ask the right questions. These are teachable skills, and I encourage mentees to sharpen them through practice, feedback, and observation.

I've closed some of my largest deals not because I had the best pitch, but because I built real relationships. I remembered a client's daughter was graduating, followed up with a handwritten note, or sent an article that aligned with their interest. These are human touches that technology can't automate—and they differentiate the good from the great.

Authenticity Is Your Advantage

In a field full of scripts and strategies, authenticity is still the most powerful tool in your toolkit. This especially applies to underrepresented professionals in sales. Many of us feel pressure to "fit in" by muting our personalities or overcompensating to prove we belong. I've done it, and still do it. But I've also learned that clients respond to realness. They don't want robots; they want people who mean what they say.

According to McCluney et al. (2019), code-switching—changing how we express ourselves to conform to dominant workplace norms—can lead to fatigue and diminished job satisfaction. When I embraced my natural tone, cultural references, and communication style, I felt lighter and more effective. Being real with clients fosters loyalty because it builds trust, and trust is the currency of sales.

I encourage sales professionals to own their voice and their story. Share your background, values, and journey when appropriate. These human elements are what help people remember you. I often share how watching my mother at The New York Times inspired my career, and how I navigate corporate America with both pride and awareness. That transparency opens doors.

A Mindset of Discipline and Growth

Sales isn't just a profession—it's a craft. To master it, you need discipline. This is the part that separates top performers from the rest. I coach new reps to treat their schedule like a business plan: block time for prospecting, follow-ups, research, and self-education. The reps who treat every day with intentionality are the ones who build momentum.

Discipline also means tracking your numbers—knowing your conversion rates, win/loss ratios, and average deal size. When you know your data, you can make informed adjustments. According to Salesforce's State of Sales report (2022), high-performing sales teams are 2.5 times more likely to use analytics to guide decision-making.

Equally important is having a growth mindset. Every loss is a lesson. Every "no" gets you closer to "yes." I've had deals fall apart after months of work—but I used those experiences to refine my process and improve. I tell every aspiring salesperson: You're not chasing perfection, you're chasing progress. Stay humble, stay hungry, and be open to feedback.

Mentorship and Paying It Forward

Perhaps the most fulfilling part of my journey is helping or mentoring others. I remember being the only person of color on my team, feeling isolated, wondering if I belonged. I've always seen the two Black person rule on most of my sales team. It is usually the max; remember this is the norm. Now, I make it a point to be visible, accessible, and real for those coming behind me.

Representation matters. When people see someone like them succeed in sales, it expands their belief in what's possible. I use formal programs and informal coffee chats, always encouraging honesty and growth. I teach the basics—how to ask better questions, how to handle objections, how to close with integrity—but I also talk about mindset, race, and navigating corporate dynamics.

Helping others become better salespeople isn't about giving them a script—it's about helping them write their own.

Sales gave me freedom, purpose, and pride. It took grit, growth, and grace to get here, and I'm still learning. But I've seen firsthand how the right mindset, discipline, and authenticity can turn potential into performance. Whether you're just starting or looking to level up, remember: your voice matters. Your story matters. And if you show up consistently with value and purpose, success will follow. I'm living proof of that—and I want to help others find their version of the dream, just like I found mine watching those sales reps at The New York Times.

Reflection Exercise: Owning Your Story

1. What parts of my story have I been hesitant to share—and why?
2. When have I doubted whether my voice mattered?
3. What is one life experience I've had that could encourage or inspire someone else?
4. How has comparison held me back from embracing my unique path?
5. What does it mean to me to lead without fame or titles?

Try This:

Write a one-page version of your story as if you were telling it to someone who needs hope. Focus on your growth, not just your achievements.

Chapter 2: More Than a Job

I learned early: unity is everything in sales.

I'm not just talking about everyone getting along or smiling in Zoom meetings. I mean real unity. The kind where people look out for each other, cover each other's blind spots, and share the wins. The kind where there's trust in every call, in every lead passed, and every hand raised in support. When a sales team is aligned—when everyone's pulling in the same direction—everything moves faster, cleaner, and better.

But here's the truth they don't always tell you in the training manuals: it only takes one person to throw that harmony off balance.

It doesn't even have to be someone loud or overtly toxic. Sometimes it's the quiet ones—the ones who gossip in whispers, side-eye every success, or pull back when the team moves forward. That kind of energy is contagious. It spreads like smoke. One bad vibe can turn teammates into rivals, and when that happens? The well is poisoned.

When Sales Were More Than Sales

I remember one of the first teams I was part of that felt different. We weren't the top office in the region. We didn't have the biggest accounts. But man, did we move like a unit. We celebrated each other. We stepped in for each other when life hit. We held each other accountable, too. When one of us was off our game, we didn't ignore it—we checked in. There was respect, and that built trust. And that trust turned into results.

We crushed it that quarter. And the one after. Not because we were the most talented, but because we were the most together.

I've worked in places where you could cut the tension with a knife— where people were so focused on outperforming each other that the customer got lost in the shuffle. And I've worked on teams where everyone believed in the mission, believed in each other, and made room for everyone to win.

Guess which ones outperformed in the long run?

The Cost of One Negative Voice

One person. That's all it takes to change the culture. One person to drain the room of optimism. One person to sit in a meeting and roll their eyes instead of contributing. That type of person doesn't just slow down sales—they shake your confidence. They make you question whether it's worth giving your best. They suck the oxygen out of progress.

And what I've learned is this: that kind of energy rarely stays contained. If leadership doesn't address it, it seeps into the whole team. Morale drops. Communication breaks. People pull back. You start holding your cards tighter because you don't trust the table anymore.

That's the opposite of unity. That's survival mode.

Character Over Commission

Here's what I've realized over the years: sales will show you who you are. Not just when you win—but especially when you lose. It shows you how you handle pressure, how you treat people when nobody's watching, and how you bounce back after rejection. And if you let it, sales can shape you into someone who leads from within, even if you're not the one with the title.

I've always believed that how you show up is more important than how much you sell. Don't get me wrong—I respect the grind. Hitting goals is part of the job. But I respect the reps who lift the team while they climb. The ones who don't hoard information. The ones who pass along leads, cover calls, and cheer loudest when someone else gets the spotlight.

That's the kind of salesperson I try to be. That's the kind of legacy I want to leave behind—not just numbers on a board, but people who say, "I was better because I worked with him."

Building Something Bigger

Leadership, I've learned, isn't just about having authority—it's about taking responsibility for the energy you bring into the room. Every time you speak, every time you choose optimism, every time you redirect a conversation from gossip to growth—you're leading. And the people around you are paying attention.

If you're on a team right now, I want you to ask yourself this: Are you adding to the alignment or pulling from it? Are you making the team better—or making it harder for the team to breathe?

I've seen what it looks like when teams operate in flow. It's powerful. And it's rare. But it's possible—when people choose unity over ego, character over clout, and purpose over petty.

Because at the end of the day, sales is more than a job. It's a proving ground. A launchpad. A place to lead, grow, and leave a mark.

And if you're going to spend 40+ hours a week doing something, why not make it mean something?

Stay Clean

So, I made a rule for myself.

Never assume.

Never gossip.

And never let someone else's opinion shape my view of a teammate.

That simple rule has saved me from so much confusion, drama, and wasted energy over the years. It's how I stay clean—even in toxic environments. Because let's be honest, not every workplace is healthy. Some places test your patience and your principles every single day. But what I've learned is this: you don't have to be messy just because the room is.

Learning the Hard Way

I didn't always have that rule. Early in my career, I fell into the same traps everyone else does. I'd hear something about a teammate, and without even thinking, I'd let it tint the way I saw them. Maybe I'd become distant. Maybe I'd be polite but cold. I thought I was being smart—"protecting my peace," as people say. But really, I was letting other people's baggage weigh me down.

Eventually, I realized that half the time, the stories I heard weren't even true. Or if they were true, they were rooted in one-sided perspectives, old grudges, or personal biases. Everyone has their own lens. Their own pain. Their own trauma. And most of the time, when people vent, they're not giving you the truth—they're giving you their version of it.

That's when it clicked for me: I'm responsible for my own mind. I get to choose what I believe. So, I stopped accepting secondhand opinions like they were facts. If I had a question or concern about someone, I went directly to them. Face to face. Heart to heart. It wasn't always easy, but it was always worth it.

The Courage to Go to the Source

People avoid confrontation because they're afraid. They don't want to make things awkward. They don't want to be disliked. But I've learned that asking questions—genuine, respectful questions—isn't confrontation. It's clarity. And clarity is freedom.

I remember approaching a colleague once after I heard they had a problem with me. I didn't accuse them or bring heat. I just asked, "Hey, I've been hearing some things. I'd rather hear it from you—are we good?"

They were shocked. Turns out, it was all a misunderstanding. That five-minute conversation cleared the air and probably saved us both months of quiet tension.

The truth is, most people don't expect you to go straight to them. But when you do—with honesty and respect—it builds a level of trust that gossip never could. Going to the source isn't just about protecting your peace. It's about practicing leadership, even when you don't have a title.

Everyone's Carrying Something

I remind myself constantly: everyone is carrying something. Pressure. Pain. Self-doubt. Childhood trauma. Relationship stress. Just because someone is cold, distant, or even rude doesn't mean they're a villain. It might just mean they're bleeding and trying to hide the wound.

But here's the key: their baggage is not mine to carry.

I can be empathetic. I can be understanding. But I don't have to inherit their negativity. I don't have to treat someone differently because of a story someone else told me. I don't have to join the whispering circle or give side-eyes during meetings. That's not leadership. That's fear in disguise.

The moment you stop carrying other people's emotional luggage is the moment you start walking lighter. And the lighter you walk, the farther you go.

Staying Clean Is a Daily Choice

There have been moments—especially in corporate environments—where staying clean felt like swimming against the tide. Gossip is casual currency in those spaces. Assumptions run wild. People take sides before they even know the full story. But that's exactly why the rule matters.

Staying clean doesn't mean being perfect. It means being intentional. It means asking yourself: "Am I adding value or adding noise?" If the answer isn't clear, take a breath. Step back. Reset. The standard you set for how you show up will influence how others show up around you.

I've worked in places where negativity was normal. Where survival meant staying silent or playing along, but I made a decision—I will not poison the space I stand in. I will not be a carrier of chaos. I will not feed division. I will lead by example, even when no one's watching.

That's staying clean.

Leadership Without a Title

You don't need a title to be a leader. Leadership is about choices. And one of the most powerful choices I made is to remain rooted in integrity when everything around me feels shaky.

I don't always get it right. I'm human. I've had moments of frustration. But I always come back to the rule that has become my anchor:

Never assume. Never gossip. Go to the source. And don't let someone else's pain become your perspective.

That's how I lead. That's how I protect my peace. That's how I stay clean.

Reflection Exercise: Leading with Integrity in Toxic Spaces

Take a quiet moment to reflect on your recent interactions in the workplace—or in any team setting. Then, answer the following questions honestly, either in a journal or just to yourself:

1. Have I ever let someone else's opinion shape the way I view a colleague?
2. What was the result of that?
3. Did I ever take the time to learn the other side of the story?
4. When was the last time I made an assumption without having all the facts?
5. How did that assumption affect my behavior or attitude?
6. Have I been part of gossip—directly or indirectly?
7. Why did I participate, and how did it feel afterward?
8. What would it look like for me to "go to the source" more often?
9. Is there a relationship in my life right now that could be healed or clarified through a direct conversation?
10. What does "staying clean" mean to me personally?
11. What one habit or mindset can I commit to in order to protect my peace moving forward?

Try This:

For one week, practice your own version of the rule:

- No assumptions.
- No gossip.
- Go directly to the source.

Write down how it changes your mood, relationships, or work environment. Then revisit this chapter and reflect on what you learned.

How Much Does Your Team Affect Your Sales? A Lot More Than You Think

Sales is often seen as a solo sport—individual quotas, personal bonuses, and one-on-one client relationships. How many times have I been driving in the car, saying to myself. I sure would be nice to be with another person today, not every day, but sometimes. The high-performing salesperson is celebrated, while the team dynamic is often ignored or underestimated. But the truth is, your team affects your sales far more than you may realize. From morale and motivation to shared resources and collective knowledge, a strong team can elevate a salesperson's performance in ways that alone cannot. Anytime I have a question about a product or service, I can reach out to another colleague or manager. Conversely, a dysfunctional or disengaged team can drag down even the most talented individual. Exploring the measurable and intangible ways that a team's dynamics impact sales performance, drawing from research in organizational behavior, psychology, and real-world sales practices, is part of being a good sales rep.

Team Dynamics as a Performance Multiplier

The performance of a sales team is not merely the sum of its parts; it is often multiplied or diminished based on how well the team collaborates, communicates, and supports one another. According to Katzenbach and Smith (2005), high-performing teams function on shared goals, mutual accountability, and deep trust. In a sales environment, this can translate into better information flow, stronger client management, and improved problem-solving. For instance, when a team shares insights about customer objections or industry trends, each member benefits—and their performance improves accordingly. Don't get too involved in conversations, making fun of members. Take it with a grain of salt and keep it moving.

Sales professionals who operate in silos may miss out on trends or opportunities that more communicative teams pick up. Remember that sometimes, as a black or minority salesperson operating within the group will have unique challenges that you must overcome to still accomplish your goals. Peer learning becomes essential in fast-moving industries. A study by Pulakos et al. (2002) found that learning from coworkers in a high-performance context boosts adaptability and sales output. Simply put, when your teammates are strong and collaborative, you are more likely to win deals, hit targets, and grow faster.

Psychological Safety and Motivation

The emotional and psychological climate within a team plays a critical role in determining how confident and focused each individual feels. Google's landmark research on effective teams found that psychological safety—the belief that one can take risks without fear of humiliation—was the most important factor distinguishing successful teams from average ones (Rozovsky, 2015). As a Buddhist, we have a monthly Discussion meeting where we talk freely about different texts. I look at sales meetings the same way. In sales where rejection is frequent and pressure is high, psychological safety can be the difference between persistence and burnout. So don't take it too seriously.

When salespeople know that their team has their back, that mistakes won't be weaponized, and that questions are welcomed rather than mocked, they're more willing to take initiative and stretch beyond their comfort zones. This directly affects their results. As Goleman (1998) notes, emotionally intelligent leaders build teams where empathy and trust drive performance. Leaders who cultivate emotionally safe environments increase team motivation—and in turn, that motivation boosts sales outcomes. Just remember that everything is not as it seems. YOU ARE NOT WHITE! If you don't drink the Cool-Aid, you will have a great career. Am I saying there is one standard for you and another for White people? Sometimes!!!

Accountability and Peer Pressure

Accountability is a double-edged sword, but in the right team setting, it becomes a performance booster rather than a stressor. When teams operate with clear standards and mutual accountability, individual salespeople are more likely to stay focused, meet deadlines, and push for excellence—not because they're afraid of management, but because they don't want to let themselves down or their peers.

Lencioni (2002) emphasizes the importance of accountability as one of the five foundations of effective teams. In high-trust environments, peer accountability strengthens discipline. I've personally seen how being part of a driven sales team—where people celebrate each other's wins and call out when someone's slipping—can raise the bar for everyone. When mediocrity isn't tolerated by your peers, it rarely survives.

Moreover, social proof plays a role: when you're surrounded by high performers, you start modeling their behaviors, processes, and work ethics. Bandura's (1977) social learning theory explains that people learn by observing others. So, if you're on a team full of disciplined, proactive salespeople, chances are you'll raise your game just by being in proximity.

Information Sharing and Efficiency

Sales move fast. Markets shift, client needs evolve, and competition adapts. In that environment, knowledge is power—and the team that shares knowledge well wins. When teams are siloed or competitive in unhealthy ways, valuable information gets trapped. But in high-functioning sales teams, knowledge is pooled, refined, and redistributed constantly.

A Harvard Business Review article by Dyer and Hatch (2006) found that collaborative knowledge-sharing significantly improves performance in teams, especially in knowledge-driven fields like consulting and B2B sales. Whether it's a great email template, a new software shortcut, or a warning about a client's hidden objections, every piece of shared information makes the team smarter—and individual salespeople faster and better prepared.

In my own career, I've seen the difference between a team that hoards information for personal advantage and one that believes "if I win, we win." The latter always outperforms in the long run. When people feel supported and informed, they spend less time guessing and more time selling.

Culture: The Invisible Hand of Success

Team culture is the undercurrent that shapes everything. It determines how people show up, how they handle setbacks, and how they support one another during crunch time. A culture of positivity, excellence, and service drives sustainable success. On the flip side, toxic cultures—where blame, fear, or competition rule—erode trust and drain energy. I have been through the highs and the lows, that's why I stay in the middle of the pack. Focused on my numbers, there to help, but at the same time staying in my lane.

Schein (2010) defines organizational culture as "a pattern of shared basic assumptions" that is taught to new members as the correct way to perceive and act. This culture either accelerates or undermines sales success. In sales, culture shows up in small moments: how people celebrate wins, how they recover from losses, and how they treat one another when quotas aren't being met. When sales are low and everyone is struggling to make their numbers, don't get baited into that negative conversation. Deflect it and stay positive with every word that leaves your mouth. Remember, it shapes your reality.

Even informal team norms—like being generous with leads, sharing scripts, or mentoring junior reps—build a culture that improves everyone's chances of winning. In today's hybrid and remote environments, culture matters even more because casual face-to-face support is no longer automatic. A strong, intentional team culture helps recreate that glue even across screens.

Your team affects your sales more than you think—perhaps more than any CRM, strategy, or script. When teams are built on trust, accountability, shared knowledge, and culture, they don't just make individuals feel good—they make them better. Sales might start with individual effort, but sustained success is always a team sport. High-functioning teams create environments where people thrive, grow, and win together. So the next time you focus on your numbers, take a minute to check your team dynamics—because who you sell with may matter just as much as who you sell to.

Chapter 3: Life on the Sales Board!

Sales is often described as a rollercoaster — a high-adrenaline ride filled with dizzying highs, frustrating lows, and brief moments of calm. But if you started your sales career during the era of physical sales boards, you know just how *visible* that ride used to be. There was no hiding in the shadows. Your name was either on the top of the board or it wasn't. It was public. It was personal. And it was powerful.

That board didn't just measure performance; it measured pride, grit, respect, and resilience. It was the scoreboard of your career — where reputations were built, and sometimes broken. Today, the boards are gone — replaced by dashboards, digital leaderboards, and Slack kudos. The game hasn't changed, but the feel of it has.

This chapter dives into what life was like when there was a sales board, and what has been gained and lost in our shift to electronic systems. More than nostalgia, this is about the psychology of performance, the culture of visibility, and the character it takes to climb back up when you're down.

The Physical Sales Board: A Culture of Visibility

The classic sales board — a whiteboard, corkboard, or chalkboard — was the centerpiece of any good sales floor. It was part scoreboard, part war memorial. Names, tallies, deals closed — all were written in dry-erase marker for the whole team to see.

Every morning, as reps walked in, they'd glance at the board. It was instinct. You couldn't help it. Whether you were on top or clawing your way from the bottom, the board reminded you where you stood.

According to Pink (2011), intrinsic motivation matters — but in sales, extrinsic motivation can be just as powerful. The board was an ever-present reminder that you were not only selling against the market, but also standing shoulder to shoulder with your peers. That competition was healthy, even when it hurt.

For some, the board created pressure. For others, it created purpose. You wanted to earn your space on that wall.

The Highs: Riding the Top of the Board

When your name was on top — bold, underlined, and possibly circled in red marker — it meant something. It wasn't just recognition; it was validation. You were the person others looked to. You were closing. You were delivering.

Being on top often meant the manager gave you a nod in the morning. Maybe even bought your lunch. You felt like you belonged. That status was earned through cold calls, long hours, and relentless follow-ups.

The dopamine rush of seeing your name on top cannot be overstated. Studies have shown that performance recognition, especially in public, boosts both individual self-esteem and team morale (Deci & Ryan, 2000). On a good day, the board could carry you. On a bad one, it could haunt you.

The Lows: When Your Name Disappears

But let's talk about the other days. The days you dread — when the ink on the board skips over your name. When the new hire passes you. When the person you mentored is now leading the pack.

It's humbling. Sometimes embarrassing. And if you're not careful, it's easy to let those days define you.

There were mornings when I'd stare at that board and think, *What am I even doing here?* I've had dry spells. I've had slumps. And I've had days when I wanted to quit. But I didn't because the board was also a teacher.

It taught patience. It taught resilience. It taught the long game. Sales boards showed you that today's bottom dweller could be next month's MVP — and vice versa. That kind of transparency, as gutting as it could be, bred humility and hope in equal measure.

The Transition: From Boards to Dashboards

Technology changed everything. CRMs like Salesforce, HubSpot, and Microsoft Dynamics became the norm. Now, data is centralized, accessible, and constantly updated in real time (Buttle & Maklan, 2019).

We log in to dashboards instead of looking at walls. We get email alerts instead of dry-erase markers. In some ways, this is a blessing. The information is more accurate. Metrics are granular. Managers can see progress down to the call and follow-up level.

But something got lost. That visceral feeling of seeing your name physically climb the board? Gone. The morning huddle around the board? Gone. The post-close marker celebration? Also gone.

Digitization has made sales more efficient — no doubt. But it's also made it quieter, more isolated. Gamification and KPIs are helpful tools, but they don't replicate the culture that the sales board created.

The Psychological Toll: Visibility and Vulnerability

Whether public or private, being measured is stressful. Sales is a performance sport. And when your numbers are visible to everyone, your performance becomes part of your identity.

Research supports this: individuals who are constantly evaluated, especially in public settings, can experience anxiety and reduced self-efficacy over time (Bandura, 1997). On the flip side, public visibility can drive higher effort and better results (Grant, 2013).

The old sales board amplified this duality. You were vulnerable and visible. Today's dashboards offer privacy, but that also removes some of the social accountability. You're still being tracked — but now, fewer people are watching. That might be a relief to some, but for high performers, it can feel like something's missing.

Lessons from the Board: What It Taught Us

Here's what the board taught me that software never could:

1. Consistency matters. It wasn't about having one great week. It was about showing up every day. That board didn't lie.
2. Failure is part of the game. Everyone gets bumped down sometimes. The key is getting back up.
3. Celebrate your wins. A close wasn't just a number — it was a marker of momentum.
4. Community counts. Sales used to feel like a team sport. The board was the scoreboard. Today, we have to be more intentional about creating that same team energy.

Reflection: Who Are You Without the Board?

Here's a question for every salesperson reading this: Who are you without the board?

Can you still find that same fire without seeing your name at the top? Can you still push through the dry weeks without that visual motivation?

Whether you're a Gen Z SDR just starting out or a seasoned AE who remembers the smell of Expo markers, you need to know what drives you. Recognition is great — but discipline is better. Public praise is sweet — but internal validation is lasting.

As the world continues to evolve, the salesperson must evolve too — blending the lessons of the past with the tools of the future.

The sales board is more than a relic — it's a reminder. A reminder of how far we've come, and how far we still have to go. Whether your numbers live on a whiteboard or a digital CRM, what matters most is what they say about you.

Are you showing up? Are you pushing through? Are you lifting others even when you're not winning? That's what the board used to show. That's what your career can still do.

Life on the Sales Board: The Numbers Never Lie

The sales board is more than a tracking tool; it's a mirror of performance, a driver of ambition, and a silent motivator in every salesroom. It explores the psychological, emotional, and professional dimensions of the sales board and how it shapes sales culture. While the top spot is sweet, no one holds it forever. Salespeople live and breathe by those numbers—sometimes they elevate, sometimes they haunt. Yet, within the obsession lies personal evolution, accountability, and the raw truth about resilience in sales.

In the sales world, few things command attention like the sales board. Whether it's digital or old-school dry erase, the board represents more than numbers—it reflects your value, your grind, and your standing. For those of us who've lived on that board, day in and day out, it's part scoreboard, part journal. But here's the truth: no one leads the board forever. That board gives, and it takes. One day, you're on top, glowing with pride. Next, you're barely hanging on.

The Psychology of the Sales Board

Sales is as much a mental game as it is strategic. The board becomes an external measurement of internal worth. According to Gino and Staats (2015), performance metrics in high-pressure environments often trigger both motivation and anxiety. Sales reps don't just compete with each other—they wrestle with their own expectations. We glance at the board in between emails, during meetings, even when pretending not to. It doesn't ask for your attention—it demands it.

This constant attention builds what psychologists refer to as "goal orientation." There are two types: performance goals (aiming to be the best) and learning goals (aiming to improve over time) (Dweck, 2006). Sales boards tend to encourage the former. And while that can lead to fierce motivation, it also brings burnout, insecurity, and unhealthy comparisons.

Being on Top: The Highs

When you're leading the board, life feels different. You walk into the office with your head high. You get nods, admiration, and sometimes envy. Your name, in bold at the top, validates the hours, the rejection, and the grind. Research on motivation by Deci and Ryan (2000) shows that public recognition satisfies a fundamental human need:

competence. In other words, being #1 isn't just about ego—it's about feeling seen and respected.

But there's a flip side. With visibility comes pressure. Every call, every email, every interaction is now an opportunity to maintain that spot—or lose it. The top is lonely, not because others resent you, but because you now have something to lose. And in sales, people are always coming for that top spot.

Falling Off: The Lows

No matter how good you are, eventually, you will drop. A deal falls through. A vacation sets you back. The market shifts. Or maybe—someone just outgrinds you. When it happens, it stings. I remember vividly the first time I dropped from the top 3 after a long run. I felt embarrassed—even though no one said a word. That's the emotional tax of the board. It can make you question everything: your skill, your strategy, your work ethic.

According to Seligman (2006), the ability to recover from setbacks—resilience—is a more accurate predictor of long-term success than talent. The board teaches that in real time. Those who stay in the game, even after the fall, develop mental toughness that no training can replicate.

What the Sales Board Teaches Us

Despite its harshness, the board offers important lessons:

1. Consistency Over Flash: One good month won't keep you there. The board teaches you to build habits, not just chase glory.
2. Humility: Even the best fall off. Success is borrowed, never owned.
3. Team Awareness: While it's easy to focus on yourself, the board shows patterns. Who's rising? Who needs help? Great salespeople lift others even while climbing themselves.
4. Adaptability: The best reps know when to change approach, switch markets, or lean into new strategies—especially when the numbers don't lie.

Sales Culture: Then and Now

The old-school sales board—erasable markers, laminated names, and clapping after a big deal—felt tangible. You could smell the ink and hear the tension. Today, digital dashboards dominate. They're efficient, real-time, and global. But something's lost in translation. The physicality of the old board made wins feel personal and failures feel intimate.

Still, the emotional energy remains. Whether on a screen or a wall, those numbers carry weight. A study by Rackham (1988) on high-performing sales teams found that consistent performance feedback—public or private—was critical to long-term success. Today's dashboards may lack the ceremony, but not the significance.

Your Turn Is Coming: Staying Grounded in the Highs and Lows of Sales

Sales is an emotional sport. Every deal is a victory, every loss a lesson. It's easy to let the highs inflate your ego or let the lows break your spirit. The importance of emotional balance in a sales-driven environment emphasizes how avoiding arrogance during success and bitterness during setbacks fosters long-term growth, character, and team culture. Grounded in personal experience and supported by research in motivation and emotional intelligence, this reflection encourages professionals to trust the journey—because everyone's turn eventually comes.

Sales is personal. It's scoreboard-driven, emotionally taxing, and incredibly rewarding. But if there's one universal truth I've learned, it's this: don't let envy take root. Don't let the highs make you arrogant or the lows make you bitter because your turn is coming. Always.

This is not just motivational talk—it's a survival strategy in a competitive space where emotions run high and ego can quietly sabotage progress. Whether you're leading the board or watching from the bottom, your mindset determines your future more than your current position does.

Envy: The Silent Underminer

It's natural to compare. You see a colleague consistently closing deals, getting recognition, making money—and a little voice whispers, "Why not me?" That voice can be motivating, but if unchecked, it grows into envy. And envy, according to Smith and Kim (2007), can quietly erode job satisfaction, team relationships, and personal performance.

Envy isn't just about wanting what someone else has. It's the belief that their success somehow diminishes your own. In sales, this shows up when you start rooting against your teammates or discrediting their wins. The problem? That energy poisons the team culture and clouds your thinking. You spend more time comparing than executing.

To stay clear-headed, I've learned to genuinely celebrate others. It takes discipline, but it's powerful. Gratitude and humility aren't just character traits—they're performance strategies. According to Emmons and McCullough (2003), employees who practice gratitude show greater resilience, stronger work ethics, and higher performance in high-pressure environments. The better you feel about others' success, the more you open yourself to your own.

Don't Let the Highs Make You Arrogant

I've been on top of the board. There's a natural swagger that comes with it—and that's okay. Confidence is fuel. But the minute you start believing you're untouchable, the fall becomes inevitable. Sales is cyclical. Success this month doesn't guarantee momentum next quarter.

Arrogance blinds you to change. You stop listening, stop learning. You begin thinking you're above coaching or that you don't need to adjust your approach. That's when performance declines.

Jim Collins (2001), in *Good to Great*, warned of the "hubris born of success"—the idea that success breeds complacency and arrogance, which ultimately leads to decline. Salespeople must remain students of the craft. The market changes, client needs evolve, and competitors innovate. Staying humble keeps you sharp and adaptable.

Leadership in these moments is key. When you're on top, ask yourself: Am I lifting others? Am I modeling the habits that got me here? Because how you act when you're winning says more about your character than how you act when you're not.

Don't Let the Lows Make You Bitter

On the flip side, when you're struggling, bitterness is a dangerous companion. The board isn't kind—it doesn't care about the deals that almost closed or the personal issues you're juggling. It just shows the numbers. And when your name is low, it can hurt. Deeply.

Bitterness creeps in as self-pity or cynicism. It whispers that the game is rigged, that your territory is weak, that leadership plays favorites. Sometimes it feels justified—but it never helps. In fact, bitterness blocks the very energy you need to climb out of the hole.

Martin Seligman (2006) describes the concept of "learned helplessness," where repeated setbacks can cause people to stop trying, believing nothing will change. But his work also introduced learned optimism—a skill where people train their minds to reframe adversity as temporary and surmountable. That's what salespeople need in the low seasons: belief that it will turn around. Because it usually does.

Your Turn Is Coming

The beauty of sales is that it resets. Every month, quarter, or fiscal year, you get a new chance. That's why I say, "your turn is coming." I've seen rookies go from last place to Presidents Club. I've watched veterans hit career highs after long slumps. The only consistent difference? They kept showing up.

Faith in the process is a discipline, even when the board shows zero. Even when the phone feels heavy and rejection is loud. You keep dialing. You keep learning. You keep showing up with integrity and energy.

Angela Duckworth (2016) defines this as grit: the passion and perseverance for long-term goals. In sales, grit beats talent over time.

You don't need to be the smartest or flashiest—you need to be the most consistent. That's how you earn your turn.

Sales is a rollercoaster. The highs can tempt your ego, and the lows can tempt your spirit. But neither should define you. The board is just a snapshot—it's not the full story. Stay grounded. Celebrate others. Reflect instead of react because your time will come. And when it does, you'll know you earned it the right way.

Chapter 4: Always Be Marketing

In the sales world, few phrases have the resonance of "Always be closing" — immortalized by the 1992 film Glengarry Glen Ross. But over the years, through countless interactions with clients, prospects, and partners, I've come to live by a different mantra: "Always be marketing." While closing is critical, marketing is what keeps the pipeline full, the brand relevant, and the trust intact. Marketing isn't just a task; it's a state of mind. Whether you're dropping off flyers, following up on leads, posting on social media, or simply showing up prepared and presentable — it all matters.

The Evolving Sales Landscape

The traditional sales cycle has evolved. In the past, sales professionals often relied heavily on cold calling and foot traffic to build their books of business. Today's buyers are more informed and more skeptical. According to HubSpot (2023), 60% of consumers prefer to learn about a product or service through online content over direct contact. This shift underscores why modern salespeople must embrace marketing as part of their daily habits. The fusion of sales and marketing, often referred to as "smarketing," reflects this evolution. If salespeople want to stay competitive, they need to think and act like marketers.

Marketing Is Momentum

Marketing creates momentum. Every touchpoint, every flyer, every email signature with a call-to-action — they all keep your name in the mix. The day you stop marketing is the day your momentum stalls. As a young sales rep, I learned that silence can kill your brand faster than a rejection. People need to see your face, hear your name, and be reminded of your value. Even when you're not actively pitching, your presence should do the talking. This is especially true in competitive industries where buyers have endless options.

Consider this scenario: Two reps pitch similar products. One walks away after the first meeting; the other leaves behind a follow-up packet, sends a thank-you email, and delivers a branded calendar the next week. Who do you think gets remembered? Who feels more professional and invested? Marketing bridges the gap between the initial conversation and the close.

Branding Yourself Every Day

Every interaction is a chance to build your brand. You may not have a personal logo or a flashy website, but your brand is in how you communicate, how you follow up, and how you show up. Your tone, timing, and consistency matter. As Keller (2021) notes, a brand is not just what you say it is — it's what others believe it to be.

When I was in the field, I treated my car trunk like a mobile office. I had brochures, pens, pop-up banners, and backup business cards. Why? Because I believed that preparation is part of the marketing process. You never know who you'll run into or when the opportunity will arise. It might be a gas station attendant who needs insurance, or a coffee shop manager who's hiring for benefits. Every moment is a marketing moment.

Digital Marketing in Sales

Modern marketing is also digital. If you're not leveraging social platforms, you're missing massive opportunities. LinkedIn, Instagram, and even TikTok have become hubs for business content. According to the Content Marketing Institute (2022), 73% of B2B marketers say social media is their most effective content distribution channel. I regularly update my LinkedIn profile not for vanity, but visibility. Clients Google you. Make sure what they find is polished and professional.

Email marketing is equally powerful. A simple newsletter or value-based email can keep you top of mind. Use tools like Mailchimp or HubSpot to automate campaigns and track engagement. These aren't just for marketing teams — they're tools for any savvy salesperson who understands the value of consistent exposure.

Old School Still Works

That said, don't underestimate the power of traditional methods. Flyers, business cards, and branded items may feel outdated, but they still work — especially in community-based industries. I've walked into barbershops and left with new clients because I dropped off a flyer or sponsored a community event. Promotional items like pens, mugs, or USB drives are tangible reminders of your presence. People use them, and when they do, they remember you.

The key is consistency. Marketing isn't a one-time event. It's a continuous process. It's the art of repetition with value. As Drucker (2008) famously said, "The aim of marketing is to know and understand the customer so well that the product or service fits him and sells itself." That level of trust and familiarity doesn't happen overnight — it's built through persistent, thoughtful marketing.

Negotiation Is Marketing Too

People often see negotiation as a hard sell — the final push. But it's actually a form of marketing. When you negotiate, you're reinforcing your value. You're articulating what makes your product worth it. You're marketing the problem you solve and the difference you make. Good negotiation isn't just about the numbers — it's about the narrative.

For example, when I negotiate with a client about plan pricing, I don't just drop numbers. I highlight outcomes. I reference similar clients who've benefited. I paint a picture of what success looks like. That's marketing — storytelling with purpose. And the better you are at this kind of marketing, the easier the close becomes.

Mindset Over Medium

At the core of "Always be marketing" is a mindset. It's not about how much money you spend or how flashy your materials are. It's about showing up every day with intention. It's about being your own ambassador, advocate, and brand manager. It's about keeping your value visible even when you're not in the room.

I once heard someone say, "Don't get ready, stay ready." That's the essence of this chapter. Marketing isn't a task you check off once a week — it's the posture you take in every interaction. Whether you're online or on-site, you are the message. Make it count.

Sales without marketing is like a car without fuel. You might coast for a while, but eventually, you'll stall. By adopting a marketing mindset, you multiply your chances of success. You create visibility, reinforce credibility, and build momentum that leads to long-term growth. So drop off that flyer. Update your profile. Share that article. Say hello. Because in a world full of noise, consistent, intentional marketing is what makes you stand out. Always be marketing.

Your Appearance and Energy Level Are Your Tools: The Power of Presence and Performance

In high-performing careers—whether in sales, leadership, or customer engagement—the most underappreciated tools are often the ones we carry with us daily: our appearance and our energy. The power of maintaining a high energy level and a professional appearance, emphasizing the psychological and strategic benefits of smiling, enthusiasm, and elevating one's presence in face-to-face interactions. Drawing from personal stories and research in psychology, business, and communication, we can examine how these human tools impact perception, improve outcomes, and help professionals stand out. Smiling is more than a gesture—it's a strategy. Energy is more than motivation—it's your currency.

I learned early in life that people watch how you show up long before they listen to what you say. Whether you're walking into a boardroom, stepping on stage, or just meeting someone new, your energy and appearance are silently announcing who you are. I grew up in the fast-paced environment of NYC and NJ, raised by a single Black mother who always made sure I understood the value of how I carried myself. Later, I found myself in rooms where I was often the only person who looked like me, and I realized something powerful: when you smile, when your energy is high, when you walk in sharp and focused—you change the atmosphere.

The Psychology of Appearance and First Impressions

I remember walking into one of my first corporate meetings after joining a new company. I had on my best navy suit, shirt crisp, shoes polished. I wasn't the most experienced in the room, but I knew one thing: I looked like I belonged. People greeted me with respect—

before I said a word. Research by Willis and Todorov (2006) supports this: first impressions are formed in less than a second, and they stick.

Appearance isn't about vanity—it's about credibility. Especially as a Black man in corporate spaces, I've always been aware that how I present myself can either open doors or reinforce assumptions. A clean look, upright posture, and a calm, confident tone go a long way in setting the tone. I may not have had the same pedigree or access as others, but I made sure my presence did the talking.

Smiling: The Universal Connector

There's a saying: "Your smile is your logo. Your personality is your business card." I've learned this to be true in rooms from downtown Miami to healthcare conferences in Chicago. Once, I was pitching a smart city initiative to local leaders and council members. It was a tense room—budget talk will do that to people. I opened with a warm smile and a quick, sincere joke about the unpredictability of city traffic. The whole room laughed. You could feel the tension drop.

Smiling is a leadership skill. It's a trust signal. Goleman (2006) writes that smiling triggers reward centers in the brain—it makes others feel good just being near you. That's not fluff—that's neuroscience. And in sales, it's gold. I've closed deals simply because people felt good talking to me. Not because I had the fanciest pitch, but because I brought the right energy and made them feel seen.

Energy as a Differentiator

There was a time I gave a keynote presentation at a community event after a 10-hour workday. I was exhausted. But I remembered what one of my mentors told me: "When you're face-to-face, turn it on." That night, I went to another level. I brought every ounce of energy I had, projected my voice, locked eyes with the crowd, and smiled like I had slept 10 hours. The result? People came up afterward saying, "You lit up the room. I felt every word."

Barsade and Gibson (2007) write about emotional contagion—how energy spreads like wildfire. I've seen it in action. Walk into a team meeting low-energy, and everyone slouches. Walk in excited, intentional, and focused? You lift the room. That's not just leadership. That's strategy.

One thing I always tell young professionals: don't just bring energy. Be aware of your energy. People are watching you more than you think. And how you show up consistently—high or low—creates your brand.

The "Turn It On" Philosophy

There's a "stage presence" I learned from doing comedy, especially watching comedians on stage. The minute I stepped onto that stage— I turned it on. That stayed with me.

In my corporate career, I've had to do the same. In sales meetings, when I walk into a room or open up Zoom, I flip the switch. It's not fake. It's focused. That's the difference. You're not pretending— you're performing with purpose. You're taking everything you are— your experience, values, energy—and putting it on display so people feel it.

Whether I'm addressing a team or meeting with city leaders, I've learned to elevate my presence. Speak with pace and passion. Be animated, but intentional. I want people to feel my belief in what I'm saying because that belief is contagious.

Burnout vs. Recharge: Protecting the Source

Now let's be real—you can't operate at 100% all the time. I've hit walls. I've walked into meetings tired, frustrated, even discouraged. But I've also learned how to protect my energy.

Stretching, staying active, eating clean—those aren't just health choices. They're performance strategies. I drink water like it's fuel (because it is), and I spend quiet time in prayer or reflection to reset my spirit. I've even learned the power of humor and music—Gospel,

R&B, Hip Hop—whatever lifts me. If I'm heading into a big day, I might throw on some Anthony Hamilton or Lecrae and let that energy rise.

You can't give what you don't have. So protect your well. Rest when needed. Prepare like a pro. Then when the lights come on—you shine.

Practical Application: Daily Tools of the Trade

Here's my go-to checklist—things I still do before key meetings, events, or presentations:

- Suit up intentionally: Know your audience and dress accordingly.
- Smile before you walk in: Set your own tone first.
- Stand tall, speak with clarity: Don't just talk—command the room.
- Check your energy: Are you bringing life or draining it?
- Connect with eye contact: Show people you see them.
- Close strong: Leave them with confidence, not confusion.

These aren't gimmicks. They're habits. They're how I've stayed relevant, persuasive, and respected in rooms I wasn't always "expected" to be in.

Your appearance and energy level aren't just accessories—they're your instruments. When you smile, when you stand tall, when you project positive energy, you're sending a signal: I came to make this moment count.

No one can control the outcome of every interaction. But you can control how you show up. And that control—especially in sales and leadership—is everything. I've lived it. I've used these tools to break through noise, build trust, and keep people engaged.

So the next time you're about to walk into a room—whether it's for a sale, a speech, or a strategy session—take a breath, square your shoulders, smile, and turn it on. Because when you bring your full presence, people listen. And they remember.

The Power of Morning Intentions: Stretching, Exercise, and Spiritual Centering

In today's fast-paced world, intentionality in our morning routine can be the deciding factor between a productive and chaotic day. The personal and holistic benefits of incorporating morning stretching or exercise two to three times a week, alongside practices like prayer or mindfulness. Drawing from real-world experience and health literature, it argues that how one starts their day can significantly impact emotional well-being, physical health, and goal orientation. Through intentional habits, individuals can re-center their lives around discipline, clarity, and purpose.

Each morning, we are given a new opportunity to set the tone for our day. For me, that often begins with a simple but transformative question: What do I want to accomplish today? Whether I'm preparing for a social event, reviewing a strategic plan at Elevance Health, or just taking care of my dog, how I start my day matters. I've found that a combination of stretching or exercise two to three times a week and morning prayer creates a rhythm that fosters clarity, strength, and inner peace. In this book, I will explore how the integration of these practices—physical exercise and spiritual centering—creates a foundation for intentional living.

The Physical Benefits of Morning Movement

Exercise doesn't need to be extreme to be effective. According to the Centers for Disease Control and Prevention (CDC, 2022), adults should engage in at least 150 minutes of moderate-intensity physical activity per week. Breaking that down into manageable sessions—like stretching or light cardio two or three times weekly—is both achievable and sustainable.

Stretching is often overlooked, yet it plays a critical role in muscle flexibility, injury prevention, and joint health. When done first thing in the morning, stretching helps shake off the stiffness from sleep, improve circulation, and stimulate the nervous system (Harvard Health Publishing, 2020). On days when I don't feel like doing a full workout, I'll opt for a 30-minute stretch session. The movements open my body, and the breathwork calms my mind.

Exercise, particularly in the morning, is also tied to increased focus and cognitive function throughout the day (Hillman et al., 2008). A brisk walk, pushups, or resistance band training before sunrise doesn't just help my body—it helps me bring energy and confidence into every room I enter, whether that's in a corporate meeting or a community forum.

Morning Intentions and Mental Focus

I have a personal rule: when I wake up, I better know what I want to accomplish. That doesn't mean I have every hour scripted, but it means I have direction. Without that, the day can slip away into distraction or reactivity. Setting an intention in the morning—whether through journaling, a mental checklist, or even a spoken affirmation—creates psychological alignment.

Research shows that setting daily goals increases self-efficacy and productivity (Locke & Latham, 2002). For me, that looks like identifying two or three key tasks I need to move forward. Sometimes it's about finishing a chapter of a book I'm writing; other times, it's making a difficult call or leading a team meeting. Whatever it is, naming it first thing gives it power.

I've also found that this discipline teaches me to be honest with myself. If I didn't meet my goal yesterday, I reflect—not to shame myself, but to recalibrate. This balance of accountability and self-grace is essential to long-term growth.

Prayer, Mindfulness, and Spiritual Alignment

Alongside physical discipline and goal setting, I believe in spiritual centering. On alternate mornings from exercise, I pray. It may be 30 minutes of prayer or simply sitting in silence with my thoughts. Sometimes I pray with music in the background—usually gospel or soft jazz—and sometimes I sit outside and listen to nature.

Prayer for me is a time of surrender and alignment. It's when I ask, "What's the purpose behind what I'm doing today?" It's not always deep or dramatic—sometimes it's just about staying humble, grateful, and grounded.

This spiritual time doesn't make life easier, but it gives me resilience. According to the American Psychological Association (2014), mindfulness and spiritual practices are associated with reduced stress, improved emotional regulation, and higher levels of life satisfaction. When combined with exercise, the benefits are multiplied: body, mind, and spirit are all activated.

Personal Anecdotes: Lessons from Routine

I remember one week when I skipped my routine. Meetings ran late, I overslept, and I told myself I'd catch up on the weekend. By Thursday, I felt disconnected. I was snapping at people, struggling to focus, and my confidence dipped. The physical neglect had a mental and emotional cost.

Then, the following Monday, I reset. I did a light stretch session, made a smoothie, and prayed for 20 minutes. That day, I felt aligned. I got through my toughest calls and handled pressure with patience. That's when I really understood: these habits are not chores—they are anchors.

Another time, I ran into a colleague who said, "Man, you always come in charged up. What's your secret?" I told him—"I get up early, I move, I pray, and I get intentional." He laughed but admitted he was struggling with burnout. We started sharing routines, and now we hold each other accountable a couple of times a week.

Building Your Own Rhythm

I often tell people not to copy my exact routine but to build their own rhythm. If you're not a morning person, start with 10 minutes of stretching and a cup of tea while you jot down your goals. If you're not religious, practice gratitude or meditation. What matters is the intentionality.

Consistency matters more than intensity. That's why I aim for 2–3 exercise sessions a week instead of daily ones that I might eventually skip. Over time, small routines become rituals, and rituals create identity. I'm no longer just someone who tries to be healthy—I am someone who honors my mind, body, and spirit before I give myself to the world each day.

Challenges and Staying Accountable

Of course, life gets busy. Travel, family obligations, work deadlines—they can all disrupt even the best routines. That's why I don't chase perfection. I build in flexibility. If I miss a morning, I try to make it up with a walk in the evening or 10 minutes of breathing at lunch.

I also stay accountable by writing down my intentions the night before and tracking my workouts and prayers in a simple journal. Seeing that record keeps me honest—and encourages me on the days I feel like quitting.

Surrounding yourself with like-minded people is another way to stay on track. Whether it's a friend who texts you after their morning run or a colleague who shares their goals, support makes the journey lighter.

Starting your day with clarity, movement, and spiritual intention isn't just about productivity—it's about living from a place of purpose. Whether it's two or three times a week or every single day, creating space in the morning for your body and soul changes everything. It transforms how you lead, how you show up, and how you handle adversity. In my life—professionally and personally—it's made all the difference.

Chapter 5: Leadership Without the Title Owning Influence Before Position

Titles don't make leaders—impact does. Over the years, I've worked under every type of leadership you can imagine: micromanagers, visionaries, quiet influencers, loud motivators, and even the "lead by absence" types. But one thing I've learned from all those experiences is this—true leadership has little to do with what's on your business card. You can lead from any seat, at any stage, with or without formal authority. And if you're in sales, you already know that influence is everything.

Leadership without the title means being someone others trust, look to, and count on—not because they have to, but because they want to. It's about showing up every day with character, clarity, and consistency.

The Myth of "I'm Not the Boss"

It's easy to fall into the trap of thinking leadership is something you earn after a promotion or a certain number of years in the company. I used to believe that myself. Early in my career, I assumed leadership came with hierarchy. But then I met someone who shattered that myth—a receptionist named Diane.

Diane had no direct reports, no corner office, and no high-level responsibilities on paper. But she was a leader. Why? Because she ran that front desk like a CEO. She knew everyone's name, noticed when people were off their game, kept confidential information locked down, and made the entire building feel like a place you wanted to be. That's leadership. Quiet, humble, and undeniable.

What Leadership Really Means

At its core, leadership is about three things: influence, responsibility, and example.

1. **Influence** – Are you moving people toward a shared goal?

2. **Responsibility** – Are you willing to own outcomes and solve problems?
3. **Example** – Do you model what you want to see in others?

John C. Maxwell (2007) put it perfectly: "Leadership is influence—nothing more, nothing less." It doesn't require permission. It requires action.

When you decide to speak up in a meeting, stay late to help a colleague, or hold your team accountable to higher standards—you are leading. And trust me, people are watching.

Sales and the Everyday Leader

Sales teaches you leadership whether you're ready or not. Every time you pitch a product, negotiate a deal, or walk into a room full of executives, you're practicing influence. But some of the most important leadership moments happen off-stage—how you treat assistants, how you respond under pressure, and how you carry yourself after rejection.

I remember one quarter where our entire region missed our numbers. Morale was low. I didn't have a managerial title, but I took it on myself to rally the team. I started each day sending short motivational texts or songs. I booked a conference room for strategy huddles—no agenda, just ideas. One teammate later told me, "You kept us from crumbling." That's when I realized leadership had less to do with power and more to do with presence.

Leading Up, Across, and Within

There are three dimensions of leadership you can step into right now:

- **Leading Up:** Anticipate your leader's needs. Solve problems before they become issues. Offer perspective without overstepping. Great leaders notice people who make their lives easier.
- **Leading Across:** Build peer relationships. Encourage others. Be the one who bridges gaps between silos. Teams thrive when someone takes the initiative to create unity.

- **Leading Within:** This is the deepest layer. It means self-awareness, self-discipline, and self-leadership. Before you lead anyone else, lead yourself.

Daniel Goleman (1995) identified emotional intelligence as the cornerstone of leadership. The most impactful leaders I know are not just strategic—they're emotionally grounded.

Character Over Clout

It's tempting to chase recognition, but influence lasts longer than applause. One of the most important leadership choices you'll make is to prioritize integrity over popularity. That means keeping your word, owning your mistakes, and doing the right thing even when no one's watching.

I once had a manager who promised the team a bonus for meeting a certain metric. We hit the mark. Corporate pushed back. Instead of hiding behind red tape, she fought for us—and found a workaround that honored her word. I learned more about leadership in that one week than in any official training

Reflection Exercise: Leadership Audit

Take a few minutes to reflect:

- Where am I already leading in my current role?
- Who do I influence regularly—intentionally or unintentionally?
- What's one way I can lead more effectively without waiting for a title?

Now write down one habit you will start this week to build your leadership muscles. Maybe it's mentoring someone new, speaking up more in meetings, or just showing up early and prepared.

Anecdote: The Team Call That Changed Everything

Years ago, I was on a tough team. Performance was lagging. People were frustrated. One Friday, I took a risk. I shared a quick presentation

I'd created—part stats, part motivation, part laughter. I told stories, challenged the team, and ended with a simple phrase: "We don't have to wait to be great."

The following week, something shifted. People were more engaged. One teammate said, "That was the first time I felt like we had a voice." I didn't have a leadership title—but that day, I led.

Closing Thoughts: Your Title Will Follow Your Influence

If you lead well without the title, the title will often find its way to you. But even if it doesn't, you've already won. Why? Because real leadership is never about control—it's about contribution. Now this book isn't only about me, it is about everyone's struggle to be better.

So, whether you're running the boardroom, managing a territory, or just showing up every day trying to do your best—don't wait for permission. Don't wait to be anointed. Show up. Speak up. Lift others. Lead.

As a woman or minority, this is especially important to do, so don't hold back!

Because the world needs more leaders who understand that leadership is not a position—it's a posture.

Everyone Has a Sales Book in Them: The Universal Nature of Sales and the Power of Results

Let's look at the universal nature of sales, arguing that everyone is involved in selling whether they realize it or not. While many believe sales is a specialized profession, sales principles apply broadly to everyday life. The pressure of sales quotas and numbers in the professional sales world, the mindset required to embrace sales skills, and how results ultimately define success. Drawing on psychology, business theory, and real-world sales practices, this book shows that sales is an essential human activity and skill set valuable beyond traditional sales roles. Every job is a sales job. If you don't make numbers, not good. If you don't do your job, not good!

Sales is often misunderstood as a narrow profession restricted to the act of exchanging products or services for money. Many people say, "Sales is not for me," perceiving it as a high-pressure, uncomfortable job best left to extroverted, persistent personalities. Yet, the truth is far more inclusive. In fact, everyone is a salesperson, whether by design or circumstance (Rackham & DeVincentis, 1999).

We constantly influence, persuade, and negotiate in daily life—from convincing a colleague to support an idea, to persuading a child to complete homework. Everyone has a sales book inside them, metaphorically speaking, and the result—the outcome of influence and persuasion—is what ultimately counts in any sales-related endeavor.

The Universal Nature of Sales

The idea that "everyone is in sales" extends beyond professional contexts into the very fabric of human interaction. Pink (2012), in his book *To Sell Is Human*, highlights that 40 million Americans are involved in sales-related activities, and virtually everyone participates in selling in some form. Whether we realize it or not, selling permeates communication, leadership, and personal relationships.

Psychologically, selling is about solving problems for others and communicating value (Cialdini, 2006). When parents encourage children to adopt good habits, or when professionals negotiate workload distribution, these are sales acts in essence—attempts to bring about change by influencing behavior. Thus, sales is less about trickery or pressure tactics and more about empathy, clarity, and problem-solving.

Sales Quotas and the Pressure of Numbers

In the professional sales world, the reality of sales quotas governs the rhythm of work. Quotas set measurable targets for salespeople to achieve within defined periods, typically monthly or quarterly (Johnston & Marshall, 2016). These numbers drive motivation and accountability, but also add stress and pressure. Salespeople live by these results, making the discipline both rewarding and demanding.

Meeting a sales quota is not merely about effort but strategic execution. Sales professionals use various techniques such as prospecting, relationship building, and negotiation to meet targets (Ingram et al., 2015). Failure to meet quotas can result in consequences such as loss of commissions or even employment. This results-driven environment sharpens skills and discipline, making sales one of the most measurable professions.

Why Some People Resist Sales

Despite the ubiquity of sales, many people resist identifying as salespeople. Some fear rejection or failure; others dislike the negative stereotypes of sales as manipulative or aggressive. These attitudes stem from misconceptions that sales is a pushy, dishonest profession (Dixon & Adamson, 2011).

However, the modern sales paradigm has shifted toward value-based selling, emphasizing honest communication and building trust (Rackham & DeVincentis, 1999). For many, the reluctance to embrace sales stems from a lack of understanding or confidence rather than inherent unsuitability.

You're in Sales, Whether You Like It or Not

One of the most important realizations in personal and professional growth is accepting that sales skills are indispensable. No matter the industry or role, influencing others is fundamental. Managers sell ideas to their teams, educators sell knowledge to students, and entrepreneurs sell visions to investors.

Understanding this expands one's view of sales from a narrow job function to a broad life skill (Pink, 2012). It means that developing sales competencies—such as communication, persuasion, empathy, and resilience—benefits all individuals in numerous contexts.

The Result Is What Counts

In sales, as in life, outcomes are the ultimate measure of success. The effort alone does not suffice without results. Companies rely on sales results to drive revenue, growth, and sustainability (Ingram et al.,

2015). For individuals, results validate the effectiveness of one's approach and open opportunities for advancement.

Results-focused thinking encourages accountability and continuous improvement. By analyzing successes and failures, salespeople refine their skills, adapt strategies, and increase effectiveness (Johnston & Marshall, 2016). This cycle of reflection and adaptation is vital not only in sales but also in personal development.

Writing Your Sales Book: Everyone Has One

The metaphor of a "sales book" suggests that everyone has a story about selling—whether literal sales or figurative persuasion. This story can be a powerful tool to reflect on one's approach to influence, lessons learned, and personal growth.

Writing a sales book, or simply documenting one's experiences in persuasion and negotiation, can clarify mindset and methods. It also reinforces the importance of authenticity, empathy, and persistence—qualities that define successful salespeople (Dixon & Adamson, 2011).

Sales is not just a profession but a fundamental human activity. Everyone sells, whether in their job, family, or social circles. The pressure of sales quotas in business sharpens the focus on results, reminding us that outcomes matter. Despite common resistance to sales, embracing the role of a salesperson empowers individuals with essential skills for life. Ultimately, the result is what counts, and everyone has a "sales book" inside them waiting to be written and lived.

Exercises for the Reader

1. Identify Your Personal Sales Moments

Take a moment to reflect on the last week. Write down three specific situations where you influenced or persuaded someone, even if you didn't realize it was "sales." These could be convincing a coworker to support your idea, negotiating plans with a friend, or encouraging a family member. For each situation, answer:

- What was your goal?
- What strategy or approach did you use?
- What was the outcome?
- How did you feel during the interaction?

2. Define Your Sales Strengths and Challenges

Create a simple two-column list. In the first column, write down your top three strengths that help you influence or persuade others. In the second column, write three areas where you feel less confident or struggle when "selling" ideas or products. Reflect on how you might build or improve those weaker areas.

3. Set a Personal Sales Goal

Whether you are in formal sales or just want to improve your influencing skills, set a measurable goal for the next 30 days. Examples include:
- Initiate and lead three conversations to persuade a colleague or friend to support a new idea.
- Practice active listening and ask open-ended questions in every meeting or interaction.
- Learn and use at least two new persuasion techniques from a sales book or article.

Write your goal clearly and note how you will track your progress.

4. Practice the "Elevator Pitch"

An elevator pitch is a short, persuasive speech you can deliver in under a minute. Write a 30- to 60-second pitch to "sell" an idea, product, or even yourself—your skills, your value, or a personal project. Practice delivering this pitch aloud with confidence, clarity, and enthusiasm.

5. Analyze a Sales Interaction

Think about a recent sales interaction you observed or experienced, whether as a buyer or a seller. Analyze the interaction by answering:
- What sales techniques were used?
- How did the salesperson build rapport?

- What objections or concerns were raised, and how were they handled?
- What could have been done better to improve the outcome?

If possible, role-play this scenario with a friend or colleague.

6. Reflect on Sales Mindset

Write a short journal entry about your feelings toward sales. Do you see sales as positive, negative, or neutral? What beliefs or experiences have shaped your view? How might changing your mindset about sales improve your personal or professional interactions?

7. Role-Play a Difficult Sales Conversation

Ask a friend or colleague to help you role-play a challenging sales conversation, such as handling rejection or overcoming objections. Prepare in advance by writing down common objections you might face. Practice responding calmly and constructively, focusing on listening and problem-solving.

8. Create Your Own Sales Book Outline

Imagine you were to write your own "sales book," telling your unique story about influence, persuasion, or negotiation. Outline the key chapters or lessons you would include. Consider personal experiences, strategies that worked, and advice you'd want to share with others.

Chapter 6: The Daily Grind

The Reality of the Daily Grind

Sales is often romanticized as a game of charisma and big wins, but the truth is far more mundane—and far more demanding. The daily grind is a real test of endurance, discipline, and mindset. It's about showing up day after day, pushing through obstacles, and making consistent progress, no matter what.

In his seminal work on grit, Duckworth (2016) argues that perseverance and passion for long-term goals outweigh raw talent in determining success. This grit is what fuels sales professionals to keep dialing, prospecting, and closing, even when external factors try to derail their efforts.

Life's Interruptions Are Non-Negotiable

The car breaks down. The doctor calls with a cancellation or emergency. Your kid is home sick. These moments demand immediate attention and can shatter even the best-laid plans. It is unrealistic to expect a perfect rhythm without disruption.

What distinguishes top performers is their preparation and ability to rebound. According to a study by the Harvard Business Review, high achievers plan for contingencies and carve out buffer time to accommodate unexpected events (Smith & Johnson, 2020). This foresight enables them to respond without losing momentum.

Planning Amid Chaos

Planning is often seen as a luxury, but in sales, it's a necessity. A strategic plan doesn't just lay out what to do—it anticipates what might go wrong and prepares solutions in advance. When life throws a curveball, a plan acts as your anchor.

Some practical planning strategies include:

• **Prioritize high-impact activities:** Identify the tasks that directly influence your sales numbers and focus your energy there.

• **Time blocking:** Reserve specific chunks of your day for prospecting, client calls, follow-ups, and administrative work. Protect these blocks from interruptions.

• **Set flexible goals:** While daily or weekly targets are important, allow yourself room to adjust in case of emergencies.

• **Built-in recovery time:** Use quieter periods to catch up or prepare for upcoming busy times.

Working Harder When You Can

When your schedule is disrupted, the instinct may be to feel defeated or fall behind. However, it is possible—and essential—to "go harder when you can." This means doubling down on effort when circumstances permit us to compensate for lost time.

For example, if you lose a morning to a family emergency, consider extending your workday or shifting tasks to the evening. Use your calendar to identify windows where extra effort can yield dividends without burning you out.

This approach aligns with the concept of strategic intensity described by Collins (2001) in *Good to Great*, where companies outperform competitors by focusing disproportionately on areas that matter most. For sales professionals, this translates into focused bursts of productivity when life allows.

The Importance of Self-Care

While the mantra of "work harder" is critical, it cannot come at the expense of self-care. Chronic stress and burnout are common pitfalls in sales careers. Ignoring your physical and mental health can lead to diminished performance and long-term consequences.

The American Psychological Association (2023) highlights that regular breaks, exercise, and mindfulness practices improve focus, resilience, and overall well-being. Balancing intense work sessions with recovery keeps you sustainable in the grind.

Strategies to Manage the Daily Grind

1. Develop a Morning Routine

Start each day with intention. Morning routines that include physical activity, meditation, or journaling can set a positive tone. According to Hal Elrod's *Miracle Morning* (2012), structuring mornings around key habits increases productivity and mindset.

2. Use Technology Wisely

Leverage sales tools and apps to automate repetitive tasks and organize follow-ups. CRM systems, calendar alerts, and email templates reduce mental load and help you focus on selling.

3. Master Time Management

Use techniques like the Pomodoro Technique or time blocking to break your day into focused intervals. This approach minimizes distractions and maximizes output.

4. Build a Support System

Lean on colleagues, mentors, and family. Communicate your needs and boundaries clearly to manage expectations during tough days.

5. Reflect and Adjust

End your day with a quick review. What worked? What didn't? Adjust your plan to improve tomorrow. Reflection fosters continuous improvement and motivation.

Real-Life Example: Overcoming the Unexpected

Consider a sales rep named Tanya, who found herself juggling a broken-down car, a sick child, and a looming quarterly quota. Instead of succumbing to stress, Tanya reached out to her manager, explained her situation, and requested flexible hours for the week.

She adjusted her daily schedule to work early mornings and late evenings when her child was asleep. She prioritized key client calls during peak hours and used her commute time for quick follow-ups via mobile. Most importantly, Tanya blocked out short breaks for self-care to maintain her energy.

By the end of the quarter, Tanya met her target—not by working harder every hour, but by working smarter during available windows and maintaining balance.

The Role of Mindset in the Daily Grind

Your mindset is the lens through which you view the daily grind. A growth mindset, as Carol Dweck (2006) describes, embraces challenges as opportunities to learn and improve rather than threats.

When life throws challenges your way, your inner dialogue can either uplift or derail you. Sales professionals who cultivate optimism and resilience bounce back faster.

Affirmations and Visualization

Positive affirmations and visualization techniques help maintain focus and motivation. Spend a few minutes daily imagining yourself overcoming obstacles and closing deals. This mental rehearsal prepares your brain to act decisively under pressure.

Embracing Imperfection

Perfectionism can paralyze action. Accepting that some days will be less productive frees you to do your best without guilt. As Brené Brown (2012) emphasizes, vulnerability and self-compassion are strengths, not weaknesses.

The Daily Grind Is a Marathon, Not a Sprint

The daily grind tests your endurance, discipline, and mindset. Life's interruptions are unavoidable, but how you prepare for and respond to them shapes your trajectory.

Plan ahead, prioritize your tasks, and go harder when you can. Balance intense work with self-care. Cultivate a resilient mindset that embraces challenges and imperfections. Remember, sales success is not about perfection every day; it's about consistent progress over time.

In the words of Winston Churchill, "Success is not final, failure is not fatal: It is the courage to continue that counts."

Sales Should Be Like the Ocean: Peaceful, Forceful, and Ever-Changing

Sales is often perceived as a high-pressure, cutthroat environment driven solely by numbers and targets. However, a more balanced and sustainable approach can be found by likening sales to the ocean—peaceful, forceful, and ever-changing. This metaphor guides sales professionals to cultivate calm confidence, harness purposeful energy, and adapt fluidly to daily fluctuations. This book explores how salespeople can incorporate this mindset to improve productivity, reduce burnout, and achieve consistent success by evolving their routines, prioritizing key tasks, and practicing self-compassion when things do not go as planned.

Sales Should Be Like the Ocean: Peaceful, Forceful, and Ever-Changing

In the fast-paced world of sales, many professionals experience relentless pressure to perform, often leading to burnout and frustration. However, adopting a perspective that likens sales to the ocean can provide a powerful framework for managing the emotional and practical challenges of the profession. The ocean embodies peace, power, and constant transformation—qualities that salespeople can emulate to cultivate resilience and effectiveness.

This book will explore three core characteristics of the ocean—peacefulness, forcefulness, and ever-changing nature—and how they apply to sales strategies and mindsets. It will also discuss the importance of evolving daily routines, prioritizing the most impactful tasks first, and embracing flexibility and self-kindness when plans go awry.

The Ocean's Peacefulness: Cultivating Calm Confidence in Sales

Salespeople often operate in environments filled with unpredictability, rejection, and the pressure of meeting quotas. This chaos can create internal stress and anxiety, undermining performance. The ocean, in its peaceful state, offers a metaphor for cultivating calm and centeredness amidst uncertainty. Just as the ocean's surface can be still and serene even when vast forces move beneath, sales professionals can learn to maintain composure and steady focus.

Mindfulness and emotional regulation techniques support this peaceful mindset (Kabat-Zinn, 2003). Salespeople who practice mindfulness are better equipped to detach from negative outcomes, such as lost deals, and avoid ruminating on past failures. This mental calmness helps preserve energy and keeps interactions with clients positive and authentic (Boyatzis & McKee, 2005). When a salesperson embodies peaceful confidence, they create a reassuring presence that fosters trust and rapport, increasing the likelihood of success.

The Ocean's Forcefulness: Harnessing Purposeful Energy in Sales

Despite its peaceful surface, the ocean is undeniably powerful. Waves crash forcefully, tides shift entire coastlines, and currents drive marine ecosystems. In sales, forcefulness translates into purposeful, directed energy—a proactive approach to achieving goals. It is not about aggression or impatience, but focused determination and consistent action.

Effective salespeople balance this forcefulness with strategic planning and persistence. Research shows that top sales performers engage in deliberate practice, honing their skills with intention and maintaining a steady pipeline of prospects (Ericsson, Krampe, & Tesch-Römer, 1993). This purposeful effort ensures progress even when immediate results are not visible.

Forcefulness also involves assertiveness in communication—confidently presenting value propositions and addressing objections without being confrontational (Turnbull & Johnston, 2003). Like the ocean waves that relentlessly shape the shore, consistent and intentional actions in sales gradually move the needle toward success.

The Ocean's Ever-Changing Nature: Embracing Flexibility and Adaptability

One of the ocean's defining qualities is its constant motion. The sea is never static; tides rise and fall, storms come and go, and currents change direction. Similarly, the sales environment is fluid, with shifting market trends, client needs, and competitive dynamics. Success in sales requires the ability to adapt to this variability.

Rigid routines and fixed mindsets often lead to frustration when unexpected challenges arise. Salespeople must cultivate flexibility, adjusting their tactics and expectations as conditions evolve (Brown & Eisenhardt, 1997). This might mean trying new outreach methods, learning about emerging customer pain points, or shifting focus to different segments.

Furthermore, embracing change reduces the fear of failure and encourages experimentation—both critical for growth in sales (Dweck, 2006). Like the ocean adjusting its course in response to the wind and moon, sales professionals who flow with change maintain momentum and seize opportunities.

Evolving Your Routine: Let Your Sales Approach Grow

Incorporating the ocean's qualities into a sales routine means allowing it to evolve. Sticking to the same habits day after day may lead to stagnation or burnout. Instead, successful salespeople regularly assess and refine their approaches based on feedback, results, and personal well-being.

For example, beginning the day with a focused, priority-driven task sets a productive tone. The concept of "eating the frog"—tackling the most important or challenging task first—aligns with ocean forcefulness and focus (Tracy, 2007). Completing high-impact activities early leverages peak energy and prevents procrastination.

Simultaneously, sales professionals should be open to adjusting their daily goals based on changing circumstances. Flexibility allows for recovery if a client cancels or a call falls through. A fluid routine minimizes stress and keeps motivation high.

Do the Most Important Thing First: Prioritization as a Sales Strategy

Prioritization is a vital sales skill. The ocean's powerful waves serve as a reminder to direct energy where it matters most. Rather than scattering efforts across low-value tasks, focusing on actions that drive revenue and relationship-building yields better results.

Time management frameworks such as the Eisenhower Matrix help distinguish urgent versus important tasks, guiding salespeople to concentrate on activities that contribute directly to their goals (Covey, 1989). For instance, preparing for a high-stakes presentation or following up on a warm lead takes precedence over administrative chores.

The Eisenhower Matrix is like the bouncer of your to-do list—it decides what gets in, what gets bounced, and what gets handed off to someone else. Designed by President Eisenhower (who knew a thing or two about getting stuff done), this 2x2 grid helps you sort tasks into four boxes: Do it now (urgent and important), Schedule it (important but not urgent), Delegate it (urgent but not important), and Delete it (neither urgent nor important—aka that 47th LinkedIn scroll).

For salespeople, it's a game-changer. Instead of drowning in emails or getting distracted by the donut box in the breakroom, you'll focus on high-value activities like closing deals, building client relationships, and finally following up with that hot lead from two weeks ago. In sales, time is money—and the Eisenhower Matrix makes sure you spend it like a boss, not like a squirrel chasing shiny distractions.

Moreover, prioritization reduces overwhelm and builds confidence. When salespeople clearly identify their "most important thing," they create daily wins that reinforce momentum and resilience.

Don't Beat Yourself Up: Practicing Self-Compassion in Sales

Sales is inherently unpredictable. There will be days when deals fall through, prospects are unreachable, or motivation dips. The ocean's ebb and flow remind us that highs and lows are natural and cyclical.

Practicing self-compassion helps salespeople cope with setbacks without internalizing failure or self-criticism (Neff, 2011). This mindset encourages viewing mistakes as learning opportunities and treating oneself with kindness.

Self-compassion supports mental health, reduces burnout, and sustains long-term career satisfaction (Breines & Chen, 2012). Rather than punishing themselves for an off day, salespeople can pause, recalibrate, and return with renewed energy—just as the ocean calms after a storm.

Viewing sales through the lens of the ocean offers a balanced and effective approach to the profession. By embodying peaceful confidence, purposeful force, and adaptable fluidity, salespeople can navigate the challenges of their work with greater ease and success. Evolving routines, prioritizing key tasks first, and practicing self-compassion help maintain resilience and sustained performance. Like the ocean, sales is a dynamic journey—sometimes calm, sometimes powerful, always changing. Embracing this metaphor empowers sales professionals to thrive amid uncertainty and continual growth.

Chapter 7: Keep Moving Forward

In the journey of sales and, indeed, life, there are days that feel like being caught in a tornado—whirlwinds of chaos that disrupt the best-laid plans and threaten to throw us off course. Phones die unexpectedly, computers crash at the worst moments, and internally, our minds wrestle with conflicting priorities, doubts, and distractions. Yet, amidst this storm, sometimes a single word from a colleague, friend, or mentor can pierce the chaos and remind us, "It's going to be okay." This chapter explores the importance of maintaining forward momentum despite setbacks, cultivating resilience, and harnessing the power of encouragement to keep moving ahead.

Understanding the Tornado Days

Every professional encounters days that seem determined to thwart progress. In sales, where momentum is critical, disruptions can feel catastrophic. Technical failures—dead phones, crashed software—are not merely inconveniences; they stall communication, delay responses, and threaten quotas. Simultaneously, internal distractions—stress, anxiety, conflicting values, or personal challenges—can fracture focus and sap energy.

Research shows that workplace stressors significantly affect productivity and mental health (American Psychological Association [APA], 2021). When multiple stressors converge, the cognitive load increases, diminishing decision-making abilities and emotional regulation (Lazarus & Folkman, 1984). Recognizing the reality of these "tornado days" is essential to developing strategies that allow one to persevere through them rather than succumb.

The Power of Support and Encouragement

One of the most powerful antidotes to difficult days is social support. According to Cohen and Wills (1985), perceived support reduces the negative effects of stress, enhancing psychological resilience. In a sales context, a timely encouraging word—a simple "You've got this" or "Keep pushing, you're doing great"—can restore motivation and perspective.

Encouragement serves not only as a morale booster but also as cognitive reframing, shifting attention away from obstacles toward solutions and possibilities (Fredrickson, 2001). Managers, peers, friends, and family members all play critical roles as emotional anchors in turbulent times. The sales floor culture that fosters encouragement often sees better performance, lower burnout, and higher retention (Grant & Parker, 2009).

Building Mental Resilience

Resilience, defined as the ability to bounce back from adversity, is foundational to "keeping moving forward" (Southwick & Charney, 2012). It involves both innate traits and learned skills. Key strategies to build resilience include:

• **Mindfulness and Meditation**: These practices increase awareness of thoughts and feelings, promoting emotional regulation and reducing reactivity (Kabat-Zinn, 2003).

• **Cognitive Reframing**: Changing the narrative from defeat to challenge encourages proactive problem-solving (Beck, 2011).

• **Routine and Structure**: Consistent habits provide stability amid chaos, anchoring the mind and body (Baumeister & Tierney, 2011).

Studies demonstrate that individuals with higher resilience experience less depression and anxiety during stressful periods, maintaining higher levels of engagement and productivity (Connor & Davidson, 2003).

The Role of Adaptability and Flexibility

Adaptability—the capacity to adjust one's approach in response to changing circumstances—is critical in sales and life. The tornado days test our flexibility and willingness to pivot. Instead of resisting change, embracing it as an opportunity for growth transforms challenges into learning experiences (Pulakos et al., 2000).

For example, when a phone dies and planned calls must be delayed, adaptable sales professionals might shift to emails, schedule follow-ups, or use alternate communication channels. This flexibility not only salvages the day but can uncover new methods that enhance future performance (Martin & Rubin, 1995).

Practical Tips to Keep Moving Forward

During tough days, practical steps can help maintain momentum:

• **Prioritize Ruthlessly**: Focus on the most critical tasks that impact sales goals. Use the Eisenhower Matrix to separate urgent from important (Covey, 1989).

• **Practice Self-Care**: Adequate rest, hydration, and brief physical activity recharge energy and reduce stress (Shanafelt et al., 2015).

• **Celebrate Small Wins**: Recognizing minor successes fosters positive emotion and motivation, sustaining effort through hardship (Amabile & Kramer, 2011).

• **Use Affirmations and Visualization**: Positive self-talk and envisioning success build confidence and prepare the mind for achievement (Bandura, 1997).

Implementing these strategies creates a toolkit to combat the unpredictability of tornado days and maintain forward progress.

Real-Life Stories of Perseverance

My phone died mid-call with a key client during an important deal. Rather than panic, I calmly switched to my iPad to continue the conversation via video chat. Later that day, when the CRM crashed, I used handwritten notes to track client details until tech support resolved the issue. Despite these hurdles, I closed the deal, attributing success to staying calm, being adaptable, and receiving encouragement from my associates.

Another example was when I was battling self-doubt during a particularly slow quarter. Daily affirmations and mentoring sessions helped me reframe failure as a learning step. That faithful persistence paid off with a record-breaking quarter soon after.

These stories highlight that setbacks are not endpoints but detours—important parts of the journey that strengthen character and sharpen skills. Try to keep the faith in the midst of defeat.

Tornado days are inevitable, but they do not have to derail us. By understanding the nature of setbacks, embracing support, cultivating resilience, and maintaining adaptability, we can keep moving forward. Practical strategies and a mindset that welcomes growth amidst adversity empower professionals not just to survive difficult days but to thrive beyond them. Remember: sometimes, all it takes is the right word at the right time to remind us that, no matter the storm, it will be okay.

Just Keep Moving Forward: Creating Your Path, Helping Others, and Staying Grounded

Life's journey rarely unfolds in a straight line. We face obstacles, misunderstandings, and moments when the road ahead seems unclear. Yet, the essence of perseverance is simple: Just keep moving. Whether your goals are personal, professional, or spiritual, the act of persistent forward motion carries a power that builds momentum, resilience, and eventual success.

Along this journey, it's vital to create your own path, even if it looks different from what others expect or understand. Helping others, especially when it goes unnoticed, shapes not only their lives but also strengthens your character. But beware—no matter how true or kind your intentions, some will misread you. This reality can shake your confidence. That's why staying grounded is key: grounded in your values, your purpose, and your vision.

This book explores these principles as a guide to living a meaningful, impactful life—one that honors both personal growth and the support of others, despite the inevitable misunderstandings along the way.

Just Keep Moving

The phrase "just keep moving" embodies the spirit of resilience. Life throws curveballs: setbacks, failures, rejections, and disappointments.

It's easy to feel stuck or discouraged when things don't go according to plan. Yet the key to progress is forward motion, however small.

Imagine a runner in a marathon who faces cramps or fatigue. They can choose to stop or slow down, but those who keep putting one foot in front of the other eventually cross the finish line. The power is in the persistence—not the speed.

In personal and professional life, moving forward might mean learning from mistakes, adjusting strategies, or simply showing up each day with the intention to improve. The journey may not be glamorous or swift, but consistent effort compounds over time.

Forward movement also creates momentum. Each step builds confidence and reveals new opportunities. The act of "just keeping moving" is an active choice against stagnation and despair. It's a declaration that no matter the challenges, you are committed to your progress and growth.

Create Your Own Path

In a world full of expectations, social norms, and comparisons, the courage to create your own path is a radical act. It requires listening deeply to your own inner voice rather than the noise of external pressures.

Many people feel compelled to follow the "road most traveled" because it's familiar or approved by society, family, or peers. But true fulfillment often lies off the beaten path. Creating your own path means defining success on your own terms, aligning actions with your values, and embracing your unique strengths and passions.

This process can be intimidating and lonely. Others may not understand your choices or may try to dissuade you from following unconventional dreams. But carving a unique path is necessary to unlock your full potential and leave a meaningful legacy.

For example, consider entrepreneurs who innovate in fields no one has explored or artists who break traditional molds. Their willingness to take risks and trust their instincts often leads to breakthroughs not only for themselves but for the communities they serve.

Creating your own path is also an act of self-respect and authenticity. It honors the individuality that makes you who you are. When you walk your own road, you are less likely to live with regret or resentment.

Help Others Even When It Goes Unnoticed

Helping others is one of the most rewarding aspects of life. Yet in a culture obsessed with recognition and validation, acts of kindness and support often go unnoticed or unacknowledged.

True generosity is not about receiving praise or thanks; it's about giving because it is the right thing to do. Helping others when no one is watching cultivates humility and strengthens your character. It builds an invisible network of goodwill that eventually circles back in unexpected ways.

Sometimes the people you help may never say thank you or may even forget your kindness. This does not diminish the impact of your actions. Small acts—like listening attentively, offering encouragement, or sharing knowledge—can ripple through lives and communities.

In fact, the value of helping others lies more in the act itself than the recognition it garners. Helping without expectation frees you from transactional relationships and deepens your connection to humanity.

Moreover, helping others nurtures empathy and compassion. It reminds you that everyone is fighting their own battles and that kindness is a language everyone understands.

There Will Always Be People Who Misread You

No matter how clear your intentions or how genuine your actions, there will always be people who misunderstand, misinterpret, or misjudge you. This can be frustrating and hurtful, but it is an unavoidable part of human interaction.

People's perceptions are filtered through their own experiences, biases, fears, and assumptions. They may project their insecurities onto you or fail to see your true character. Sometimes, jealousy or competition distorts how others view your success or choices.

Rather than internalizing others' misreading, it's crucial to maintain clarity about who you are and why you act as you do. Misunderstandings are often a reflection of the other person's state, not your worth or intentions.

Expecting everyone to see you perfectly is unrealistic and leads to disappointment. Instead, focus on being authentic and consistent. Over time, those who matter will recognize your true character, even if others do not.

It helps to develop emotional resilience by not taking misjudgments personally. When criticism or misreading arises, respond with grace and keep your attention on your path and values.

Stay Grounded

Staying grounded means staying connected to your core — your values, your purpose, and your truth — regardless of external chaos or pressure.

In a world of constant change and noise, it's easy to get swept up in distractions, doubts, or comparisons. Staying grounded provides a stable foundation to navigate life's uncertainties with calm and confidence.

Grounding practices vary but often include mindfulness, reflection, spiritual connection, and strong relationships. Taking time to check in with yourself regularly helps you remain centered and aligned with your goals (Katzenbach, J. R., & Smith, D. K. (2005)).

When you are grounded, you can better handle criticism, setbacks, and the unpredictability of life. You make decisions rooted in integrity rather than fear or external validation.

Moreover, staying grounded cultivates patience. It reminds you that success and fulfillment are not instant but develop over time with consistent effort.

The journey of life is a continuous process of movement, creation, service, understanding,

and grounding. To just keep moving is to embrace resilience and hope, no matter what challenges arise. To create your own path is to honor your individuality and courageously pursue what matters most to you. To help others even when it goes unnoticed is to live generously and compassionately, planting seeds of kindness without expectation. To accept that there will always be people who misread you is to build emotional strength and maintain authenticity despite misunderstanding. And to stay grounded is to anchor yourself in your values and purpose so you can navigate life's storms with clarity and peace.

By integrating these principles, you cultivate a life of meaning and impact — one that is uniquely yours and richly connected to the world around you. So take the next step. Keep moving. Your path is yours to create.

Chapter 8: The Real Obstacles

More Than Just External Challenges

When you think about obstacles in sales, what usually comes to mind? Rejection from clients? Market downturns? Fierce competition? Sure, those are real challenges. But the biggest battles often happen inside (The Sales Insights Lab, 2021). They are silent, hidden, and personal. Sometimes your own body, mind, or emotions become the toughest barriers.

I know this well. Medication that dries out your mouth, fatigue that

saps your energy, or anxiety that makes you second-guess every word you say—these are the real obstacles. They don't announce themselves like a bad market report. They don't disappear when you close your laptop. Yet, they impact every call, every meeting, every pitch.

In this chapter, I'll share how I confronted these invisible challenges and learned to manage them. More importantly, I'll offer strategies you can use when the hardest opponent in the room is yourself.

1. Physical Obstacles: The Body Can Be Your Worst Enemy

One thing that caught me off guard was how physical issues affect sales performance. Sales is communication—talking, listening, reading cues. When your mouth is dry from medication, your throat feels tight, or your voice sounds weak, it can throw off your confidence and clarity.

For example, many medications cause dry mouth, a condition called xerostomia (Villa, A., Connell, C. L., & Abati, S., 2015). It may seem minor, but try pitching a client with a parched mouth. The discomfort makes you rush your words or stumble over sentences. It's frustrating.

How to manage physical obstacles:

- Stay hydrated. Keep water within reach during calls and meetings. Sip frequently.

- Use lozenges or gum. Sugar-free gum or lozenges stimulate saliva flow and soothe dry mouth.

- Practice breathing and vocal exercises. This can help strengthen your voice and control nervousness.

- Adjust your schedule. If possible, plan your toughest calls during times you feel physically better.

- Consult your doctor. Sometimes medication adjustments or alternatives can reduce side effects.

Your body is your instrument. If it's not cooperating, sales become harder. Recognize these issues and treat your body with care.

2. Mental and Emotional Obstacles: The Battle Within

Sometimes, the hardest obstacle isn't physical—it's mental. Self-doubt, anxiety, and negative thoughts can undermine your efforts long before you dial the phone.

The voice inside your head can be brutal: "What if they say no again?" "Maybe I'm not cut out for this." "I'm just wasting my time." This internal chatter chips away at your motivation and focus (Geers, A. L., Wellman, J. A., & Lassiter, G. D., 2009).

Mindset is everything.

When I first encountered anxiety in sales, I thought it was a weakness. But I learned it's normal. Every salesperson experiences fear or doubt at some point. The difference is how you respond.

Strategies to overcome mental obstacles:

- Reframe your thoughts. Instead of "I might fail," say, "Every call is a chance to learn."

- Use affirmations. Positive self-talk can build confidence: "I am prepared," "I add value," "I can handle rejection."

- Practice mindfulness and meditation. These techniques help calm your mind and improve focus.

- Set realistic goals. Break big tasks into smaller steps so you don't feel overwhelmed.

- Seek support. Talk to mentors, coaches, or peers who understand the pressure and can offer encouragement.

Your mindset shapes your results. Cultivate resilience and compassion for yourself.

3. Emotional Fatigue: The Hidden Drain

Sales is emotionally draining. Every "no" feels personal; every objection can bruise your confidence. Over time, emotional fatigue can creep in silently, leading to burnout (Duckworth, A., 2016).

It's like running a marathon with no water stations—your energy depletes, your pace slows, and your enthusiasm fades.

How to recognize emotional fatigue:

- Feeling tired even after rest

- Losing interest in calls or clients

- Becoming irritable or impatient

- Struggling to concentrate or stay positive

How to combat it:

- Take breaks. Step away regularly to recharge.

- Celebrate small wins. Acknowledge progress, no matter how small.

- Maintain work-life balance. Spend time with family, friends, or hobbies.

- Practice self-care. Exercise, eat well, and get enough sleep.

- Know when to ask for help. Professional counseling or coaching can provide tools to manage stress.

Don't ignore emotional fatigue. It's a real obstacle that can stop you from performing at your best.

4. Internal Resistance: When You're Your Own Worst Enemy

Sometimes, the biggest obstacle is procrastination or self-sabotage. Maybe you delay calls because you're afraid of rejection. Maybe you talk yourself out of opportunities before you start.

Internal resistance is tricky because it disguises itself as comfort or avoidance (Duckworth, A., 2016). But deep down, you know it's holding you back.

How to push through internal resistance:

- Identify triggers. When do you procrastinate? What thoughts or feelings come up?

- Create routines and habits. Structure reduces decision fatigue and increases consistency.

- Commit publicly. Share your goals with others for accountability.

- Use the "5-minute rule." Start a task for just five minutes; often, momentum builds and you keep going.

- Celebrate progress. Reward yourself for following through.

The obstacle isn't the task—it's you resisting. Awareness and discipline can break this pattern.

5. Finding Strength in Vulnerability

Opening up about internal struggles isn't easy. In a culture that values strength and success, admitting to challenges feels risky.

But vulnerability is powerful. Sharing your obstacles creates connection and support. It also models authenticity, which clients and colleagues respect.

I found that being honest with my team and mentor helped me gain perspective and practical advice. It also reduced the pressure I put on myself.

If you're struggling, consider talking to someone you trust. You might be surprised how common your experiences are.

6. Real-Life Stories: Overcoming Internal Obstacles

Story 1: Sarah's Dry Mouth Battle

Sarah was a top-performing sales rep until medication caused constant dry mouth. She started avoiding calls and felt her confidence slip. After consulting her doctor and adopting hydration and vocal exercises, she regained her energy and voice. Today, she still manages symptoms but no longer lets them define her.

Story 2: James's Anxiety Breakthrough

James struggled with anxiety before every client meeting. The fear of rejection was paralyzing. He started practicing meditation and cognitive reframing. Slowly, his anxiety lessened, and his sales numbers improved. He now coaches others on managing mental obstacles.

Story 3: Mia's Emotional Fatigue Recovery

Mia loved sales, but burnout hit hard. She was exhausted, disengaged, and unhappy. Taking a short leave, focusing on self-care, and setting boundaries helped her return stronger. She now prioritizes balance and encourages her team to do the same.

7. Practical Exercises: Building Internal Strength

Try these exercises to develop resilience and overcome internal obstacles:

- Daily check-in: Rate your physical, mental, and emotional state on a scale of 1–10. Notice patterns and adjust accordingly.

- Affirmation journal: Write three positive affirmations each morning and repeat them throughout the day.

- Mindfulness break: Spend five minutes focused on your breath or surroundings to reset your mind during stressful moments.

- Goal chunking: Break your daily sales tasks into 3–5 small, manageable actions.

- Reflection: At day's end, write down one challenge you faced and how you responded. Celebrate your effort.

The Invisible Battle Is Worth Fighting

The real obstacles in sales aren't always visible. They live inside—your body, your mind, your heart. They challenge your voice, your courage, and your will.

But these obstacles don't have to stop you. Awareness, self-care, mindset shifts, and support are powerful tools. Every time you overcome an internal hurdle, you grow stronger and closer to your goals (Cunningham, C., 2024, October 14).

Remember, selling isn't just about products or quotas. It's about pushing through the parts of yourself that want to quit. It's about showing up even when the path isn't easy.

So, if your mouth feels dry or your mind feels heavy, take a breath. Keep moving. The real victory is in the fight itself.

I Push to Free Up Time for Events: Embracing Flexibility and Forward Planning

In today's fast-paced world, time is often our most precious commodity. Managing time effectively not only improves productivity but also enhances our quality of life. For me, pushing to free up time for events is a fundamental strategy to maintain balance and nurture meaningful connections. Whether it's a personal gathering, a professional meeting, or simply an opportunity to recharge, I make it a priority to carve out moments in my schedule. Yet, life isn't always predictable. Weather interruptions, unexpected delays, or shifting priorities challenge my plans. When faced with these obstacles, I adapt. I adjust with flexibility. And I always prepare for the next day — planning my schedule thoughtfully and intentionally. Regardless of whether I have appointments lined up, I get out there. I show up. This mindset drives my daily rhythm and builds resilience. Activity creates momentum for an appointment, a lead, a phone call, or even your next sale. Cause and effect, baby!

The Importance of Prioritizing Events

Events, whether social or professional, serve as essential anchors in our lives. They foster relationships, build community, and provide vital breaks from routine. I recognize that time spent at events is not just "time away" from work or obligations; it is an investment in my well-being and growth. To prioritize these experiences, I push myself to free up time, often rearranging other less critical tasks to make space.

This approach requires discipline and conscious decision-making. I regularly review my calendar to identify activities that may not yield significant value and either delegate, postpone, or eliminate them. This pruning process enables me to protect time for events that enrich my life. The effort is well worth it because events are opportunities for learning, networking, celebration, and relaxation.

Flexibility in the Face of Weather Challenges

Despite careful planning, sometimes nature has other ideas. Inclement weather can disrupt travel plans, outdoor events, or even the simple motivation to leave the house. The weather is an uncontrollable factor that tests our flexibility. When rain, storms, or extreme heat interfere with my agenda, I don't view it as a failure. Instead, I adjust my approach.

If an outdoor event is canceled, I seek alternative indoor gatherings or postpone the activity. If traveling is unsafe, I reschedule or use the time productively in other ways. This flexibility prevents frustration and helps me maintain momentum. By preparing mentally to adapt, I stay grounded and positive, no matter the weather's whims.

Planning for Tomorrow: A Habit of Preparedness

Planning ahead is a cornerstone of effective time management. Each day, after finishing my current responsibilities, I take deliberate time to prepare for tomorrow. This practice includes reviewing my calendar, setting priorities, and anticipating potential obstacles.

By visualizing the upcoming day's events and appointments, I can arrange tasks in a logical order and allocate time realistically. Planning reduces the stress of uncertainty and boosts confidence. It also creates a buffer to handle unexpected changes gracefully. When I plan ahead, I sleep better knowing that I am ready.

Showing Up Regardless of Appointments

One of the core principles I live by is the discipline of showing up — regardless of whether I have formal appointments or not. Some days, my calendar might be wide open with no scheduled meetings. Other days, back-to-back commitments fill every minute.

On days with no appointments, I still get out there. I use the time to engage with my community, explore new opportunities, or invest in personal development. This could mean attending networking events, volunteering, or simply going for a walk to clear my mind.

The act of showing up cultivates presence and builds momentum. It breaks the inertia of idleness and encourages continuous forward motion. Even without a fixed agenda, the commitment to be active, visible, and engaged propels me toward my goals.

Overcoming Internal Resistance and External Barriers

Freeing up time for events and showing up consistently is not always easy. Internal resistance, such as fatigue, self-doubt, or procrastination, can slow progress. External barriers, including work demands, family obligations, or transportation challenges, also complicate efforts (Johnston, M. W., & Marshall, G. W. (2016).

To overcome these hurdles, I rely on a combination of mindset shifts and practical strategies. I remind myself of the bigger picture — why these events matter. I set realistic goals and celebrate small wins. I communicate with stakeholders about my availability and boundaries to manage expectations.

Importantly, I cultivate patience and self-compassion. Some days will be harder than others. Allowing myself grace during setbacks prevents burnout and maintains motivation over the long haul.

The Role of Discipline and Consistency

Discipline is the engine that powers this entire process. Pushing to free up time, adjusting when necessary, planning ahead, and showing up all require consistent effort. Discipline does not mean rigidity; it means commitment to core values and long-term vision.

I develop routines that support this lifestyle, such as weekly calendar reviews, daily reflection, and accountability partnerships. These habits build structure without sacrificing flexibility. (Johnston, M. W., & Marshall, G. W. (2016). Over time, consistency creates momentum that carries me through challenges and opportunities alike.

Reflection: The Impact of This Approach on My Life

Since adopting this proactive and adaptive approach to time and events, I have noticed significant improvements in my personal and professional life. Relationships have deepened as I prioritize quality time with family, friends, and colleagues. My stress levels have diminished because I feel more in control of my schedule. Opportunities for growth and new experiences have increased because I make the effort to engage actively.

Moreover, the practice of adjusting to weather or unexpected obstacles has enhanced my resilience. Instead of feeling thwarted, I see challenges as chances to be creative and resourceful. The habit of planning for tomorrow brings clarity and focus, allowing me to start each day with purpose.

Ultimately, this lifestyle reflects a commitment to living intentionally — making time for what matters, staying flexible in the face of change, and being fully present in each moment.

Expanding on Key Themes

The Psychological Benefits of Flexibility

Adapting to weather or unforeseen changes is more than just a logistical skill; it offers psychological benefits. Flexibility reduces anxiety by preventing a fixation on rigid plans. When we accept that change is inevitable, we open ourselves to new possibilities and reduce resistance.

Scientific research supports the idea that psychological flexibility correlates with well-being, resilience, and better stress management. By embracing adjustment, I align my mindset with healthy coping mechanisms that support both mental and emotional balance.

Techniques to Free Up Time Effectively

Freeing up time for events often requires deliberate time management strategies. Here are some techniques I apply:

- Time blocking: Allocating specific chunks of time for priorities, including events.

- The Eisenhower Matrix: Prioritizing tasks based on urgency and importance to avoid wasting time on trivial matters.

- Delegation: Entrusting others with tasks that do not require my direct involvement.

- Saying no: Politely declining requests or invitations that conflict with key events or goals.

- Batch processing: Grouping similar tasks together to reduce switching costs and increase efficiency.

These strategies empower me to control my calendar proactively rather than reacting passively to external demands.

The Value of Daily Planning Rituals

Daily planning rituals are foundational to staying organized and focused. Some components of my routine include:

- Reviewing my calendar and to-do list the night before.

- Setting 3–5 key priorities for the next day.

- Preparing materials or information needed for appointments.

- Anticipating obstacles and planning contingencies.

- Visualizing a successful day ahead.

These small steps foster mindfulness and preparedness, turning abstract goals into actionable steps.

The Power of Showing Up

Showing up consistently, even on days without appointments, strengthens commitment and momentum. This principle is often discussed in personal development circles as a key to success.

Showing up:

- Builds discipline and confidence.

- Opens doors to serendipitous opportunities.

- Reinforces identity as a proactive and engaged individual.

- Provides structure to the day, preventing aimlessness.

- Enhances visibility in professional and social circles.

Whether it's attending informal events, participating in community activities, or simply being physically present, showing up matters.

Pushing to free up time for events is an intentional act of prioritization that enriches my life. When weather or other obstacles arise, I adjust with flexibility rather than frustration. Planning ahead ensures I approach each day with clarity and purpose. Regardless of appointments, I get out there, embracing the discipline of showing up consistently.

This approach reflects a mindset of proactive engagement with life's opportunities and challenges. It strengthens my resilience, fosters meaningful connections, and promotes continuous growth. Above all, it affirms the belief that how we use our time shapes our experience and defines who we are.

Chapter 9: Consistency Wins

One day, you make a sale at a doctor's office. The next day, you don't close a single deal. On some days, it feels like the world is against you — the phone doesn't ring, the emails go unanswered, and the rejections pile up. But on other days, the right connection happens. A client says yes, a referral comes through, or a carefully targeted mailer gets a positive response. You keep going. You send out mailers, knock on doors, follow up with prospects, ask for referrals, and keep marketing yourself. Because over time, all those small efforts add up. That's the power of consistency.

The Myth of Overnight Success

Many people dream of a "big break" — a moment where everything changes overnight. The truth is, success rarely happens that way. When you look closely at people who seem to have "made it," you often find years of consistent effort behind their achievements.

Consistency means showing up, day after day, whether you feel motivated or not. It means sticking to your plan, learning from failures, and making adjustments, but never giving up. The sales world is full of ups and downs, but those who maintain steady effort will ultimately come out ahead.

Why Consistency Matters

Consistency creates momentum. Imagine (Kouzes, J. M., & Posner, B. Z. (2017). Imagine you're pushing a heavy boulder uphill. At first, it's slow going. You might only move it a few inches in an hour. But if you stop every few minutes, the boulder will roll back. If you keep pushing steadily, even if slowly, eventually it will reach the top.

In sales, every call you make, every email you send, and every networking event you attend builds momentum. It might not pay off immediately, but over weeks and months, the small actions start to compound. A call you made two months ago might lead to a referral today. The flyer you distributed last week might generate an appointment tomorrow. The key is to keep the boulder moving, no matter how small the progress seems.

Building Trust and Relationships Over Time

Sales isn't just about a single transaction. It's about building trust. (Dweck, C. S. (2006). Trust takes time. It doesn't happen instantly when you hand over a business card or make a quick pitch. It's earned through repeated interactions, reliability, and showing genuine interest in your customer's needs.

Consistent communication is one way to build that trust. Following up regularly, providing useful information, and staying at the top of mind means your prospects are more likely to turn to you when they're ready to buy.

The Role of Routine

Creating a consistent daily routine is one of the most powerful tools for long-term success. Set a schedule for prospecting, follow-ups, and marketing activities, and stick to it. This doesn't mean rigidly following the same plan every single day without flexibility, but it does mean having a dependable structure to your work.

For example, you might decide that every morning from 9 a.m. to 11 a.m. is dedicated to making cold calls. The afternoon might be for responding to emails and setting appointments. Regularly sending mailers could be scheduled for the first week of each month. A routine like this helps ensure that important activities don't get neglected, even when other distractions arise.

Overcoming the Low Days

The truth is, some days will be tough. You'll face rejection, stalled deals, or simply a lack of response. On these days, it's tempting to slow down, lose motivation, or even quit. But that's exactly when consistency matters the most.

When you persist through the hard times, you develop resilience. You learn to separate yourself from the outcome of a single day and focus on the bigger picture. You trust that your ongoing efforts will eventually pay off. That mindset is a huge competitive advantage.

Leveraging Small Wins

Every sale, every referral, every positive interaction — no matter how small — is a win. Celebrate these wins. Recognize that they are evidence that your consistent effort is working.

Tracking your progress can help here. Keeping a simple journal or spreadsheet of your daily and weekly activities and results allows you to see patterns and growth over time. When the days feel long and discouraging, reviewing these wins reminds you that your work is not in vain.

Consistency in Marketing

Marketing is another area where consistency is critical. Sending out mailers, posting on social media, attending community events — these things rarely generate instant sales. But they build awareness and credibility in your market.

If you send out mailers once, you might not get much response. But if you send them consistently every month or quarter, people begin to recognize your name and your message. When they hear they need your product or service, you'll be top of mind.

Asking for Referrals Every Time

One of the most powerful habits you can develop is consistently asking for referrals. After a successful sale or positive interaction, ask your customer if they know anyone else who might benefit from your service.

Many salespeople hesitate to ask for referrals, worried about imposing or seeming pushy. But the reality is that most people are happy to help when asked at the right time. Make it a natural part of your process. (Brevet Group. (2023). Over time, referrals can become a major source of business growth.

The Compound Effect

Consistency works like compound interest in finance. Just as small deposits add up to a significant amount over time, small daily actions in sales accumulate to large results.

Take this example: If you make 10 calls a day, 5 days a week, that's 50 calls a week, or 200 calls a month. Even if your close rate is low, those calls can lead to a steady stream of leads and sales. If you stop making calls after a week or two, that pipeline dries up quickly.

Tools to Help Stay Consistent

Technology offers many tools to help maintain consistency:

• CRM software: Track contacts, follow-ups, and sales opportunities so nothing falls through the cracks.
• Email scheduling tools: Plan marketing emails and follow-ups in advance.
• Calendars and reminders: Schedule time blocks for key activities and set reminders.
• Journals or apps: Record daily wins, lessons, and challenges.

Using these tools can reduce the chance of forgetting important tasks and keep you on track.

Personal Discipline and Motivation

Consistency is a test of personal discipline. It requires you to show up and do the work regardless of how you feel. Motivation fluctuates, but discipline can carry you through.

Many successful salespeople develop habits to stay disciplined:

• Setting daily goals.
• Starting work at the same time each day.
• Taking care of their health to maintain energy.
• Having accountability partners or mentors.

Developing your own discipline strategies will pay off in the long run.

The Role of Mindset

Your mindset plays a huge role in maintaining consistency. Viewing challenges as opportunities to learn, rather than failures, helps you keep going. (Cespedes, F. V. (2014). Believing that small daily efforts matter fuels persistence.

When you focus on the process — the habits and routines — rather than just the outcome, you feel more in control and less overwhelmed. This growth mindset is a critical ingredient in consistent success.

Real-Life Example: The Doctor's Office Sale

Let's revisit that opening example: You make a sale at a doctor's office one day. Maybe you spent weeks calling, emailing, and visiting offices before finally reaching the right person at the right time. That sale didn't happen by accident — it was the result of consistent effort.

The next day, you might not make a sale. But you keep following up. You send another mailer. You call other prospects. That persistence sends a message: you're reliable, professional, and serious.

Long-Term Vision

Consistency is easier when you keep your long-term vision in mind. Know why you're doing the work. Maybe you want financial freedom, to support your family, or to build a business you're proud of.

Having a clear purpose fuels your perseverance when progress seems slow. Keep reminding yourself of the big picture, and use that to power your daily consistency.

Reflection Questions

1. What daily habits can you develop to stay consistent in your sales efforts?
2. How do you currently handle days when nothing seems to go right? How can you improve your resilience?
3. Are you leveraging referrals as part of your consistent sales process? How might you make asking for referrals a natural habit?

4. What tools or routines could you implement to better track and maintain your marketing efforts?
5. How does keeping a long-term vision help you stay consistent when short-term results are disappointing?

Journaling Prompt

Write about a time when consistency paid off in your life or work. What small, steady actions led to a significant result? How did it feel to keep going even when progress was slow? What lessons can you take from that experience to apply moving forward?

Consistency wins. It's not about making a big sale every day or closing every deal on the first try. It's about showing up, putting in the work, and trusting the process. Over time, your efforts compound and build momentum. Whether it's sending mailers, asking for referrals, or following up with prospects, keep going. Your consistent actions will create success — one small step at a time.

The 80/20 Rule Is Real: Unlocking the Power of Focus and Consistency

In today's fast-paced world, many people struggle to balance the overwhelming demands of work, personal life, and self-improvement. They find themselves constantly busy but often feel like their efforts don't translate into meaningful results. This experience is common because not all work yields equal outcomes. The 80/20 Rule, or Pareto Principle, helps clarify this by revealing a simple but powerful truth: roughly 80% of results come from 20% of efforts. (Koch, R. (2017). Understanding and applying this principle can transform how we approach tasks, priorities, and productivity. This book explores the 80/20 Rule, how to identify the crucial 20%, and why consistent action on that focused work leads to lasting success.

What Is the 80/20 Rule?

The 80/20 Rule originates from Vilfredo Pareto, an Italian economist who, in the late 19th century, observed that 80% of Italy's land was owned by 20% of the population. Since then, this principle has been seen in many fields: 80% of sales come from 20% of clients, 80% of complaints come from 20% of customers, and 80% of profits come from 20% of products.

It's a general rule of thumb—not a strict formula—but it reveals a consistent truth: results are not equally distributed. A small number of inputs often produce a large portion of the outputs.

The takeaway? Don't work harder—work smarter. Focus on the vital few tasks that drive real results. The remaining 80%—the trivial many—can drain time and energy with little to show for it.

Why the 80/20 Rule Matters

The 80/20 Rule matters because it breaks the myth that effort always equals results. Many people believe if they work harder or longer, success will follow. But effort on the wrong things leads to burnout and frustration.

Adopting the 80/20 mindset helps individuals and teams focus on what truly moves the needle. For instance, a salesperson might realize that just a few clients bring in most of their revenue. By nurturing those relationships, they can earn more while working more efficiently.

Finding Your Vital 20%

Identifying your 20% means taking time to reflect and observe what truly creates value. Here's how:

1. Track and Analyze Your Activities
Start by logging your daily work. Use a time tracker or journal for one to two weeks. Then review what led to real results—revenue, momentum, growth, or satisfaction.
Chances are, you'll notice patterns: a few tasks, clients, or conversations delivered most of the payoff. (Koch, R. (2017).)

2. Ask Key Questions
- What tasks create the most value?
- Which clients contribute the most revenue or referrals?

- What actions consistently lead to results?
- Which responsibilities feel like time-wasters?

Use these insights to refine your focus.

3. Prioritize Ruthlessly

Once you know your high-impact work, protect it. Use tools like the Eisenhower Matrix to separate what's urgent from what's important. Block time for your most critical tasks and reduce distractions.

Doing a Little of Everything vs. Focusing Deeply

The 80/20 Rule isn't about ignoring the other 80% entirely. Some of those tasks still matter—they just don't drive results.

A well-rounded approach helps. Spend the bulk of your time on your most valuable efforts, but set aside time for necessary maintenance: admin work, emails, or networking. The goal is to stay sharp without drifting from what truly matters.

The Power of Consistency

Identifying your top 20% is the first step. The next step is consistency.

That means showing up for that work every day. Not just when you're motivated. Not just when it's easy. The results compound over time when you commit to your high-value efforts with regularity and discipline

Why Consistency Matters:

- **Builds Momentum:** Small, focused actions accumulate over time to create substantial progress.
- **Improves Skills:** Repeated effort in high-impact areas sharpens expertise and efficiency.
- **Creates Habits:** Consistency transforms intentional action into automatic behavior.
- **Drives Results:** Steady work on what matters delivers compounding returns.

Without consistency, even the best insights about focus remain theoretical.

Real-World Examples of the 80/20 Rule

Sales and Marketing

Sales professionals often find that 20% of their prospects or clients generate 80% of their income. The Pareto Principle encourages focusing on building relationships with that critical group, customizing solutions, and providing excellent service. Meanwhile, less profitable leads get less time but are not ignored entirely.

In marketing, 20% of campaigns might produce 80% of leads or conversions. Tracking metrics closely helps marketers double down on the campaigns that yield the best ROI.

Time Management

Many people discover that 20% of their daily tasks produce 80% of their productive output. For instance, answering emails may feel urgent but yield little impact compared to deep work sessions focused on a key project. By scheduling blocks of uninterrupted time for critical work, professionals boost productivity dramatically.

Personal Development

When learning new skills, 20% of concepts or techniques often provide 80% of practical value. Language learners, for example, find that mastering the most common 1,000 words allows them to understand a majority of everyday conversations. Focusing on the essentials first accelerates learning.

Overcoming Challenges in Applying the 80/20 Rule

Despite its clear benefits, the 80/20 Rule is not always easy to apply:

1. Difficulty in Identification
Sometimes the vital 20% isn't obvious. It takes data, patience, and

experimentation to discover which activities truly matter. People might misjudge what's important due to biases or external pressure.

2. Fear of Neglecting the 80%
Ignoring 80% of tasks can feel risky. For example, skipping certain meetings or reports might cause anxiety about missing details or displeasing others. Learning to say no and delegate effectively is necessary.

3. Inconsistent Application
Without discipline, people might revert to busywork or multitasking, diluting focus. Building routines and accountability helps maintain consistency.

Practical Tips to Apply the 80/20 Rule Today

1. **Audit Your Week:** Identify which 20% of activities produced 80% of your progress or satisfaction.
2. **Set Priorities:** Focus daily effort on those high-impact tasks first.
3. **Limit Multitasking:** Concentrate on one vital task at a time for deeper work.
4. **Say No More Often:** Protect your time by declining low-value requests.
5. **Automate or Delegate:** Offload trivial tasks to free energy for important work.
6. **Review Regularly:** Reassess your priorities every week or month to stay on track.
7. **Be Patient:** Results compound with time and consistent focus.

The 80/20 Rule is more than a productivity hack; it is a mindset that reveals the power of focus and consistency. By understanding that 80% of results come from 20% of effort, we are encouraged to find our vital few tasks and pursue them relentlessly while maintaining balance.

Doing a little of everything with consistency ensures that progress continues across all areas without losing sight of what truly moves the needle. When you apply the 80/20 Rule thoughtfully and persistently, you unlock more time, energy, and success in work and life.

Chapter 10: Final Thoughts: Why Not You?

As we come to the close of this journey together, I want to leave you with some final thoughts—simple yet powerful ideas to carry forward. This book, this conversation, isn't about perfection. It's not a manual for flawless success or a guarantee that every step will be easy or smooth. Instead, it's about persistence: showing up day after day, continuing to push forward even when the odds seem stacked against you.

It's about honoring your story—the unique experiences that have shaped who you are—and respecting your hustle, the hard work and determination you bring to the table every day. It's about recognizing your purpose and living with intention, no matter what your circumstances might be.

You don't need a fancy title to lead others. You don't need fame or fortune to make a difference. You simply need perspective. And it's that perspective I hope to have shared with you here.

So, why not you? Why not now? The future is waiting. Keep going. Keep selling. Keep believing.

1. The Power of Persistence Over Perfection

One of the most important lessons I want to emphasize is that perfection is not the goal. Too often, people hold themselves back because they feel they must be perfect before they start or that every effort must be flawless to count. This mindset creates a barrier, a fear of failure or judgment, that stops progress before it begins.

Persistence, on the other hand, is about commitment and endurance. It's about showing up again and again, even when things don't go as planned. It's about learning from mistakes, adapting, and refusing to quit.

Think about the most successful people you know. Almost none of them started perfect. Many struggled, failed, and faced rejection. But what set them apart was their persistence. They kept moving forward despite setbacks, trusting that every effort brought them closer to their goals.

2. Honoring Your Story

Your story is your foundation. Every challenge, triumph, lesson, and setback has contributed to who you are today. Honoring your story means embracing your past without shame or regret and using it as fuel for your future.

Too often, people try to distance themselves from their beginnings or feel embarrassed about their struggles. But your journey is unique and valuable. It gives you perspective, empathy, and strength. When you share your story, you connect with others on a deeper level and inspire them to overcome their own challenges.

Your story is also a source of authenticity. People are drawn to genuine leaders—those who are real and relatable—not to perfect, untouchable personas. By owning your story, you demonstrate courage and resilience.

3. Hustle: The Daily Grind That Changes Everything

Hustle isn't just about working hard; it's about working smart, with passion and consistency. It's the daily commitment to do whatever it takes—within reason—to move closer to your goals.

Hustle looks different for everyone. For some, it means making calls, sending emails, or learning new skills. For others, it means showing up on tough days, maintaining discipline, and keeping faith in the process.

It's important to recognize that hustle without rest or balance can lead to burnout. Honoring your hustle also means taking care of yourself physically, mentally, and emotionally. Find a rhythm that allows you to give your best without sacrificing your well-being.

4. Purpose: Your North Star

Purpose is the reason you get up in the morning. It's the deeper meaning behind your work and actions. Without purpose, even the most impressive achievements can feel hollow.

Finding your purpose doesn't require grand gestures or world-changing missions. Sometimes, purpose is as simple as providing for your family, serving your community, or improving one life at a time.

When you lead with purpose, your hustle becomes meaningful. It fuels resilience and helps you navigate challenges because you know your work matters. Purpose anchors your decisions and guides your priorities.

5. You Don't Need a Title to Lead

Leadership is often misunderstood as a position or status. But true leadership is about influence, integrity, and action. You don't need a corner office or a fancy title to lead.

Every day, you have opportunities to lead: by example, through kindness, by standing up for what's right, or by encouraging others. Leadership starts with self-leadership—taking responsibility for your actions and growth.

When you embrace this truth, you realize your potential to impact those around you, regardless of your role or job description. Leadership is accessible to everyone willing to step up.

6. Fame and Recognition Are Not Prerequisites for Impact

In a culture obsessed with fame and social media, it's easy to equate visibility with value. But making a difference doesn't require a spotlight. Often, the most meaningful impact happens quietly, behind the scenes.

Helping a colleague, mentoring a young person, showing up for your community, or simply doing your job with excellence can ripple outward in ways you might never see.

Focus on making real, positive contributions rather than seeking approval or applause. Your work matters, even if it's not always recognized.

7. Perspective: The Lens That Shapes Your Reality

Perspective is how you interpret your experiences, challenges, and opportunities. It shapes your attitude, resilience, and choices.

When faced with setbacks, perspective helps you see obstacles as learning moments rather than failures. It encourages gratitude for progress and motivates you to keep going.

Developing perspective requires reflection and mindfulness. Take time to pause, assess, and adjust your outlook. Surround yourself with positive influences who uplift and challenge you to grow.

8. Keep Going: The Journey Is Yours

The path ahead will not always be smooth. There will be obstacles, doubts, and days when you want to quit. **But keep going.**

Every step forward, no matter how small, adds up. The difference between those who succeed and those who give up often boils down to perseverance.

Remember why you started. Remember your purpose, your story, and your vision. Keep pushing through the tough moments—they are often the most transformative.

9. Keep Selling: Believe in Your Value

If you're in sales—or any role that requires you to present ideas, products, or yourself—**keep selling.** This isn't just about transactions; it's about belief.

Believe in what you offer, believe in your ability to help others, and believe in your own potential. That belief will come through in your interactions and build trust.

Sales is about connection and problem-solving, not just closing deals. Keep refining your craft, listening to your clients, and adapting. Persistence in selling leads to long-term success.

10. Keep Believing: Faith in Yourself and the Process

Belief is the foundation of everything you do. **Believe in yourself, even when others doubt you.** Believe in the process, even when results aren't immediate.

Faith sustains you through uncertainty. It fuels hope and courage. Keep believing that your efforts matter, that you are growing, and that your goals are within reach.

Final Charge: Why Not You?

So, why not you? Why not now?

You have everything you need inside you to lead, to hustle, to persist, and to succeed. **Your story is valuable. Your purpose is clear. Your perspective is powerful.**

Don't wait for permission or perfect conditions. **Step into your power today.** Lead where you are. Work with intention. Believe with conviction.

This book is a starting point, a spark. The real work happens now—in your daily actions, your mindset, and your commitment to keep moving forward.

You can do this. You are meant for this.

Reflection and Action Steps

Before you close this book, take a moment to reflect:

- What parts of your story are you ready to own and honor?
- Where in your life can you lean into persistence rather than perfection?
- How can you lead today without waiting for a title?

- What is one small step you can take now to move closer to your purpose?
- How will you maintain belief and perspective through challenges?

Write down your answers. Commit to at least one action that honors your hustle and your potential.

Closing

Thank you for joining me on this journey. I hope these words inspire you to keep going, keep selling, and keep believing in yourself. Your future is bright, and the world needs what only you can offer.

Why not you?

Why not now?

This is it!

References

- Brevet Group. (2023). *21 Mind-blowing sales statistics*. https://www.thebrevetgroup.com/sales-training-statistics
- Cespedes, F. V. (2014). *Aligning strategy and sales: The choices, systems, and behaviors that drive effective selling*. Harvard Business Review Press.
- Goleman, D. (2006). *Emotional intelligence: Why it can matter more than IQ*. Bantam Books.
- Rackham, N. (1988). *SPIN selling*. McGraw-Hill.
- Blount, J. (2017). *Sales EQ: How ultra-high performers leverage sales-specific emotional intelligence to close the complex deal*. Wiley.
- Gitomer, J. (2018). *The Little Red Book of Selling: 12.5 Principles of Sales Greatness*. Bard Press.
- Sales Insights Lab. (2021). *Sales statistics: What top performers do differently*. Retrieved from https://www.salesinsightslab.com/sales-statistics
- Edelman. (2019). *2019 Edelman Trust Barometer Special Report: In brands we trust?* Harvard Business Review. Retrieved from https://hbr.org
- CSO Insights. (2018). *Sales enablement study: Sales coaching*. https://www.csoinsights.com
- Livingston, R. (2021). *The conversation: How seeking and speaking the truth about racism can radically transform individuals and organizations*. Currency.
- McCluney, C. L., Robotham, K., Lee, S., Smith, R., & Durkee, M. (2019). The costs of code-switching. *Harvard Business Review*. https://hbr.org/2019/11/the-costs-of-codeswitching
- Dixon, M., & Adamson, B. (2011). *The challenger sale: Taking control of the customer conversation*. Portfolio/Penguin.
- Gardner, W. L., Cogliser, C. C., Davis, K. M., & Dickens, M. P. (2011). Authentic leadership: A review of the literature and research agenda. *The Leadership Quarterly*, 22(6), 1120–1145. https://doi.org/10.1016/j.leaqua.2011.09.007

- Salesforce. (2022). *State of Sales Report* (5th ed.). https://www.salesforce.com/resources/research-reports/state-of-sales/

- Sinek, S. (2009). *Start with why: How great leaders inspire everyone to take action*. Portfolio.
- Bandura, A. (1977). *Social learning theory*. Prentice Hall.
- Dyer, J. H., & Hatch, N. W. (2006). Relation-specific capabilities and barriers to knowledge transfers: Creating advantage through network relationships. *Strategic Management Journal, 27*(8), 701–719. https://doi.org/10.1002/smj.543
- Goleman, D. (1998). *Working with emotional intelligence*. Bantam Books.
- Katzenbach, J. R., & Smith, D. K. (2005). *The wisdom of teams: Creating the high-performance organization*. HarperBusiness.
- Lencioni, P. (2002). *The five dysfunctions of a team: A leadership fable*. Jossey-Bass.
- Pulakos, E. D., Arad, S., Donovan, M. A., & Plamondon, K. E. (2002). Adaptability in the workplace: Development of a taxonomy of adaptive performance. *Journal of Applied Psychology, 85*(4), 612–624. https://doi.org/10.1037/0021-9010.85.4.612
- Rozovsky, J. (2015). The five keys to a successful Google team. *re:Work*. https://rework.withgoogle.com/blog/five-keys-to-a-successful-google-team/
- Schein, E. H. (2010). *Organizational culture and leadership* (4th ed.). Jossey-Bass.
- Bandura, A. (1997). *Self-efficacy: The exercise of control*. W.H. Freeman.
- Buttle, F., & Maklan, S. (2019). *Customer relationship management: Concepts and technologies* (4th ed.). Routledge.
- Deci, E. L., & Ryan, R. M. (2000). The "what" and "why" of goal pursuits: Human needs and the self-determination of behavior. *Psychological Inquiry*, 11(4), 227–268. https://doi.org/10.1207/S15327965PLI1104_01

- Grant, A. M. (2013). *Give and take: Why helping others drives our success.* Viking.
- Pink, D. H. (2011). *Drive: The surprising truth about what motivates us.* Riverhead Books.
- Dweck, C. S. (2006). *Mindset: The new psychology of success.* Random House.
- Gino, F., & Staats, B. R. (2015). *Why organizations don't learn.* Harvard Business Review, 93(11), 110-118.
- Kouzes, J. M., & Posner, B. Z. (2017). *The leadership challenge: How to make extraordinary things happen in organizations* (6th ed.). Jossey-Bass.
- Rackham, N. (1988). *SPIN Selling.* McGraw-Hill.
- Seligman, M. E. P. (2006). *Learned optimism: How to change your mind and your life.* Vintage.
- Collins, J. (2001). *Good to great: Why some companies make the leap and others don't.* HarperBusiness.
- Duckworth, A. (2016). *Grit: The power of passion and perseverance.* Scribner.
- Emmons, R. A., & McCullough, M. E. (2003). Counting blessings versus burdens: An experimental investigation of gratitude and subjective well-being in daily life. *Journal of Personality and Social Psychology,* 84(2), 377–389.
- Seligman, M. E. P. (2006). *Learned optimism: How to change your mind and your life.* Vintage.
- Smith, R. H., & Kim, S. H. (2007). Comprehending envy. *Psychological Bulletin,* 133(1), 46– Content Marketing Institute. (2022). *B2B Content Marketing: Benchmarks, Budgets, and Trends.* Retrieved from https://contentmarketinginstitute.com
- Drucker, P. F. (2008). *Management: Tasks, Responsibilities, Practices.* HarperBusiness.
- HubSpot. (2023). *The State of Marketing Report.* Retrieved from https://www.hubspot.com/marketing-statistics

- Keller, K. L. (2021). *Strategic Brand Management: Building, Measuring, and Managing Brand Equity* (5th ed.). Pearson Education.
- Barsade, S. G., & Gibson, D. E. (2007). *Why does affect matter in organizations?* Academy of Management

- Perspectives, 21(1), 36–59. https://doi.org/10.5465/amp.2007.24286163
- Brown, S. P., & Lam, S. K. (2008). *A meta-analysis of relationships linking employee satisfaction to customer responses.* Journal of Retailing, 84(3), 243–255. https://doi.org/10.1016/j.jretai.2008.06.001
- Willis, J., & Todorov, A. (2006). *First impressions: Making up your mind after a 100-ms exposure to a face.* Psychological Science, 17(7), 592–598. https://doi.org/10.1111/j.1467-9280.2006.01750.x
- American Psychological Association. (2014). *Mindfulness meditation: A research-proven way to reduce stress.* https://www.apa.org/news/press/releases/2014/10/mindfulness
- Centers for Disease Control and Prevention. (2022). *How much physical activity do adults need?* https://www.cdc.gov/physicalactivity/basics/adults/index.htm
- Harvard Health Publishing. (2020). *The importance of stretching.* https://www.health.harvard.edu/staying-healthy/the-importance-of-stretching
- Hillman, C. H., Erickson, K. I., & Kramer, A. F. (2008). *Be smart, exercise your heart: Exercise effects on brain and cognition.* Nature Reviews Neuroscience, 9(1), 58–65.
- Locke, E. A., & Latham, G. P. (2002). *Building a practically useful theory of goal setting and* Goleman, D. (1995). *Emotional intelligence: Why it can matter more than IQ.* Bantam Books.
- Maxwell, J. C. (2007). *The 21 irrefutable laws of leadership: Follow them and people will follow you.* Thomas Nelson.
- *task motivation: A 35-year odyssey.* American Psychologist, 57(9), 705–717.
- Cialdini, R. B. (2006). *Influence: The psychology of persuasion* (Rev. ed.). Harper Business.
- Dixon, M., & Adamson, B. (2011). *The challenger sale: Taking control of the customer conversation.* Portfolio.

- Ingram, T. N., LaForge, R. W., Avila, R. A., Schwepker, C. H., & Williams, M. R. (2015). *Sales management: Analysis and decision making* (8th ed.). Routledge.
- Johnston, M. W., & Marshall, G. W. (2016). *Sales force management: Leadership, innovation, technology* (12th ed.). Routledge.
- Pink, D. H. (2012). *To sell is human: The surprising truth about moving others*. Riverhead Books.
- Rackham, N., & DeVincentis, J. (1999). *Rethinking the sales force: Redefining selling to create and capture customer value*. McGraw-Hill.
- American Psychological Association. (2023). *Stress management*. https://www.apa.org/topics/stress

- Brown, B. (2012). *Daring greatly: How the courage to be vulnerable transforms the way we live, love, parent, and lead*. Gotham Books.
- Collins, J. (2001). *Good to great: Why some companies make the leap... and others don't*. HarperBusiness.
- Elrod, H. (2012). *The miracle morning: The not-so-obvious secret guaranteed to transform your life (before 8AM)*. Hal Elrod International.
- Smith, R., & Johnson, K. (2020). Planning for unpredictability: The secret weapon of high achievers. *Harvard Business Review*, 98(4), 45-53.
- American Psychological Association. (2021). *Stress in America 2021: Stress and health disparities*. https://www.apa.org/news/press/releases/stress/2021
- Amabile, T., & Kramer, S. (2011). *The progress principle: Using small wins to ignite joy, engagement, and creativity at work*. Harvard Business Review Press.
- Bandura, A. (1997). *Self-efficacy: The exercise of control*. W. H. Freeman.
- Baumeister, R. F., & Tierney, J. (2011). *Willpower: Rediscovering the greatest human strength*. Penguin Press.
- Beck, J. S. (2011). *Cognitive behavior therapy: Basics and beyond* (2nd ed.). Guilford Press.

- Cohen, S., & Wills, T. A. (1985). Stress, social support, and the buffering hypothesis. *Psychological Bulletin*, 98(2), 310–357.
- Connor, K. M., & Davidson, J. R. (2003). Development of a new resilience scale: The Connor-Davidson Resilience Scale (CD-RISC). *Depression and Anxiety*, 18(2), 76–82.
- Covey, S. R. (1989). *The 7 habits of highly effective people*. Free Press.
- Fredrickson, B. L. (2001). The role of positive emotions in positive psychology: The broaden-and-build theory of positive emotions. *American Psychologist*, 56(3), 218–226.
- Grant, A. M., & Parker, S. K. (2009). Redesigning work design theories: The rise of relational and proactive perspectives. *Academy of Management Annals*, 3(1), 317–375.
- Lazarus, R. S., & Folkman, S. (1984). *Stress, appraisal, and coping*. Springer.
- Martin, M. M., & Rubin, R. B. (1995). A new measure of cognitive flexibility. *Psychological Reports*, 76(2), 623–626.
- Pulakos, E. D., Arad, S., Donovan, M. A., & Plamondon, K. E. (2000). Adaptability in the workplace: Development of a taxonomy of adaptive performance. *Journal of Applied Psychology*, 85(4), 612–624.
- Shanafelt, T. D., Noseworthy, J. H. (2017). Executive leadership and physician well-being: Nine organizational strategies to promote engagement and reduce burnout. *Mayo Clinic Proceedings*, 92(1), 129–146.
- Southwick, S. M., & Charney, D. S. (2012). *Resilience: The science of mastering life's greatest challenges*. Cambridge University Press.
- Villa, A., Connell, C. L., & Abati, S. (2015). **Diagnosis and management of xerostomia and hyposalivation**. *Therapeutics and Clinical Risk Management*, 11, 45–51. https://doi.org/10.2147/TCRM.S76282.

- Geers, A. L., Wellman, J. A., & Lassiter, G. D. (2009). Dispositional optimism and engagement: The moderating role of goal orientation. *Personality and Individual Differences, 47*(8), 851–856. https://doi.org/10.1016/j.paid.2009.07.027.
- Cunningham, C. (2024, October 14). *The surprising self-sabotage among sales professionals – and how to overcome it. Sales & Marketing Magazine.* Retrieved from Sales & Marketing Magazine website.
- Koch, R. (2017). *The 80/20 principle: The secret to achieving more with less* (Updated ed.).

www.ingramcontent.com/pod-product-compliance
Lightning Source LLC
Chambersburg PA
CBHW061233070526
44584CB00030B/4105